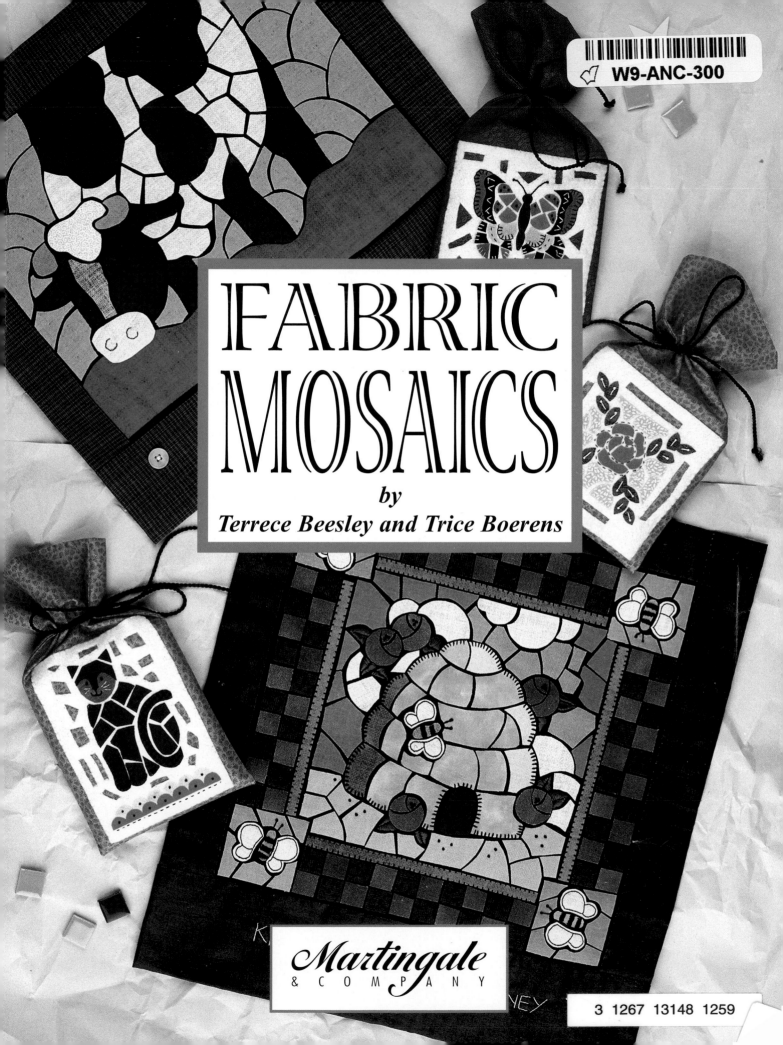

FABRIC MOSAICS

by
Terrece Beesley and Trice Boerens

Martingale
& COMPANY

Martingale & Company
PO Box 118
Bothell, WA 98041-0118 USA

Printed in the United States of America
04 03 02 01 00 99   6 5 4 3 2 1

Credits

Artist..Terrece Beesley
Artist...Trice Boerens
Designer ....Cherie Hanson
Editor ....Margaret Shields Marti

Fabric Mosaics
© 1999 by Terrece Beesley and Trice Boerens

Library of Congress Cataloging-in-Publication Data

Beesley, Terrece.
    Fabric mosaics / by Terrece Beesley and Trice Boerens.
        p.   cm.
    "Pastimes"—CIP cover.
    ISBN 1-56477-267-5
    1. Appliqué—Patterns.   2. Embroidery.   3. Mosaics.
I. Boerens, Trice.   II. Title.
TT779.B42   1999
746.44'5041—dc21   98-49857
                                                              CIP

Contents

Basic Instructions 4

CHAPTER ONE

Sunflower Coaster 8
Teacup Coaster 10
Framed Blue Vase 12
Framed Summer Bouquet 17
Monogram Heart Pillow 23
Monogram Diamond Pillow 26
Hearts & Flowers Sampler 29

CHAPTER TWO

Sheep Wall Hanging 36
Beehive Wall Hanging 40
Spotted Cow Wall Hanging 45
Butterfly, Floral, & Cat Gift Bags 49
Framed Sunshine 57

CHAPTER THREE

Table Runner 61
Woodland Squirrel Pillow 62
Garden Rabbit Pillow 67
Nesting Pair Pillow 71
Rainbow Trout Pillow 75
Striped Bass Pillow 77

CHAPTER FOUR

Framed Apples 82
Framed Grapes 85
Framed Cherries 87
Framed Pears 90
Orange Pillow 92
Lemon Pillow 95

Basic Instructions

You are guaranteed to be a success with this appliqué process! It's very fast and easy. Do two pieces seem crowded? Trim one edge. Are a few pieces too far apart? Trace one or two of them again and cut them a little larger.

Begin by acquainting yourself with the properties of paper-backed fusible web. The smooth side, the paper side, is for tracing patterns using an ordinary pencil. On the rough side you can feel the crystals that melt when they come in contact with the heat of the iron.

All the patterns in the book are facing the right way, that is, the way they appear in the finished project.

Preparing the Pattern Pieces

First, trace the entire pattern onto tracing paper, using a heavy pencil line. You will use this pattern twice—first to trace the pieces, and later as an overlay to guide you when fusing. Turn the tracing paper pattern face down. Place the fusible web, paper side up, over the pattern. With fusible web, you must trace the pattern in reverse in order to have it facing the right way after fusing. Trace a pattern piece onto the paper; the pattern is backwards at this point.

Working with the pattern still face down, trace pieces that are to be cut from the same fabric (such as green leaves) in groups, allowing about ¼" between pieces. (The colors on the pattern pieces in the book indicate pieces to be cut from the same fabric. Some fabric groups are numbered to indicate the sequence in which they should be fused. You may want to color and number your pattern, too.) Cut the web in one piece, about ½" away from the pencil lines. You are ready to fuse a piece or group of pieces to fabric.

Know your iron. A few experiments and you can tell how many seconds and what temperature setting give you the best results. It doesn't take very much heat, about 2 or 3 seconds. Fusing is like preparing pasta; don't overcook it.

Place the rough side of the web against the wrong side of the fabric (if it has a wrong side). Iron for 2 or 3 seconds until your pattern piece is fused to the fabric. At this point, your pattern piece is still backwards from the photo and from the pattern in the book (Diagram 1).

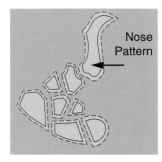

Pattern pieces are backwards against wrong side of fabric.

Diagram 1

Preparing the Templates

A key to success is using templates as directed in each project. The template is just tissue paper with a shape from the pattern traced, then cut out. It helps "frame" the space as you begin to appliqué the pieces in the design. The template works with the pattern overlay to guide you in placing the pattern pieces.

Pinning the Layers Together

Place the template over a piece of background fabric, pinning the corners (Diagram 2). Then place the pattern overlay, right side up, over the template and fabric, aligning the template and the pattern so they match (Diagram 3).

Pin the pattern overlay along the top edge only. The pattern overlay will remain in the same place throughout the appliqué process, but the template is temporary.

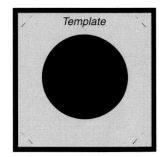

Diagram 2

Three layers: felt, tracing paper template, and pattern.

Diagram 3

Fusing the Pieces

Cut out the pattern pieces along the pencil lines. It's best to cut only two or three pieces at a time; they tend to look very similar to each other once cut out. Peel the paper backing from the web. Place the cutout fabric piece, right side up, on the felt, using the template and the pattern overlay as your guide (Diagram 4). Now the piece will correspond with the photo and the pattern. Fuse in place.

Diagram 4

Continue to fuse a few pieces at a time, following the pattern overlay (Diagram 5). When the area outlined by the template has been completed, remove the template and throw it away. Continue to fuse pieces until the design is complete.

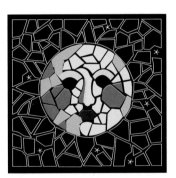

Remove template after center pieces are in place.

Diagram 5

When the pieces have cooled, check to see that all are adhering well, especially on the edges.

That's all there is to it! This is the process for making all the appliqué designs in this book. We suggest starting with the Sunflower Coaster so you can see how fast and easy this process is.

Helpful Hints

• If the pattern piece depends upon straight edges, such as a border strip or checkerboard pieces, use a ruler to draw the lines, making sure they are parallel, instead of tracing the pattern by hand.

• Trace all the pieces that use the same fabric close together onto the web. Then cut out the whole piece of web containing those pieces. Fuse the whole piece to the fabric and cut out the individual pieces as you are ready to use them.

• You may turn the pattern and web in any direction you want when working with solid colors. In fact, variety in the grain of the fabric enhances the finished product. If the pattern in the fabric is important to the design, such as stripes in border pieces, plan carefully as you trace the pieces onto the web.

• In most cases when the instructions call for a print, the design is small and does not contrast much with the background color; for example, the fabric color is mottled and when the small pieces are cut out, they appear to be from different fabrics. The variations add to the interest of the design.

• When the embroidered design on a project contains lettering or is more detailed than you wish to draw freehand, use a water-soluble marker or transfer pencil. For either tool, follow the manufacturer's instructions and experiment before using it on a project. To use the transfer pencil, trace the lettering from the pattern in the book, using a heavy pencil line. Then turn the pattern upside down. Trace the lettering onto tracing paper using the transfer pencil; it will be backwards. Place the transfer-pencil pattern, right side up, where you want it on the fabric. Iron. On dark fabrics, use dressmaker's chalk or white artist's tracing paper.

Stitches

Back Stitch

Bring the needle up at 1, down at 2, up at 3. Go back down at 1, and continue in this manner.

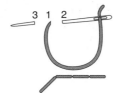

Cross Stitch

Each single cross is made of two stitches forming a cross. Large areas or rows may be worked by first stitching across the row from left to right. Complete the crosses by working back across the row from right to left. All top stitches should slant in the same direction.

Buttonhole Stitch

This stitch is worked from left to right. Bring the thread out at 1. Insert the needle at 2, and bring it out at 3, stitching over the first stitch. Insert the needle at 4 and repeat.

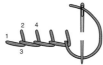

Chain Stitch

Bring the needle up at 1, hold down a small loop of thread, and insert the needle at 2. Bring the needle up at 3 and insert it at 4, guiding the needle over the loop and securing the previous loop with the loop just formed. Repeat, securing each loop with the next to form a chain. Take a small stitch over the end of the last loop to secure the end.

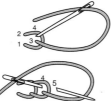

Couching

Use these simple stitches to anchor a length of floss or ribbon to fabric.

French Knot

Bring the needle up at 1 and wrap floss once (or twice) around the shaft of the needle. Swing the point of the needle clockwise and insert into fabric at 2. You can change the size of your knot by varying the strands used or wrapping more times.

Long Stitch

Bring the needle up at 1, down at 2 to complete the stitch.

Satin Stitch

Bring the needle up at 1 and down at 2, making parallel stitches. Repeat to fill a desired area.

Star Stitch

Bring the needle up at 1, down at 2, up at 3, and down at 4. Continue in this manner until the entire star shape is formed.

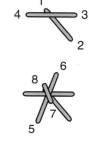

Stem Stitch

Bring the needle up at 1, down at 2, up at 3, and down at 4, keeping the thread to the right of the needle.

Sunflower Coaster

Materials needed for each coaster:

Scraps of cotton fabric in these colors: purple, gold,
    light blue, and green
Large scrap of fabric in contrasting color for binding;
    matching thread
6" x 6" piece of black felt
White embroidery floss
Scraps of fusible web
Tracing paper; pencil

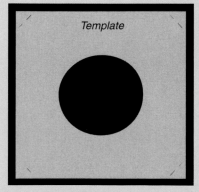

Diagram 1

Make the Sunflower Design

1. Using the pattern on page 11, trace the edges of the flower center and the outside edges of the design onto tracing paper. Cut out the center, leaving the rest of the paper intact. Place the template over the felt, with the outside edges parallel to the edges of the felt (Diagram 1).

2. Make the pattern overlay; see Basic Instructions. Use the overlay to trace all the pattern pieces onto fusible web. Pin the overlay to the felt and leave in place throughout the appliqué process.

3. Cut out fabric pieces for the purple flower center, working with just a few pieces at a time. Peel off the paper backing and place on the felt, fusible side down, using the template as a guide to placement. Fuse the pieces. Repeat to complete the center of the flower (Diagram 2). Remove the template.

4. Cut out and fuse the gold petals (Diagram 3).

5. Cut out and fuse the green leaves, then the light blue background.

Embroider the Details

1. Using 2 strands of white floss, cross-stitch the purple flower centers in a random pattern (Diagram 4).

2. Make a single ½"-long stitch in each leaf with 2 strands of white floss.

Bind the Edges

1. Cut 2"-wide bias strips from contrasting fabric. Piece as needed to make a 25"-long strip.

2. Trim the felt to 5" x 5", keeping the design centered and the edges parallel to the design edges.

3. Stitch the binding to the right side of the felt ½" from the edges, stopping ½" from the corner; backstitch (Diagram 5). At the corner, fold the binding at a right angle. Resume stitching with a backstitch ½" from the edge (Diagram 6). Repeat at each corner.

4. Fold the edge of the binding under and then fold to the back, making a ½"-wide binding. Slipstitch to the back, covering the stitching line and mitering each corner.

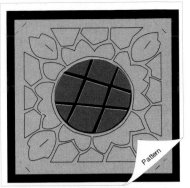

Diagram 2

Diagram 3

Diagram 4

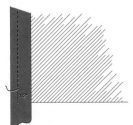

Diagram 5

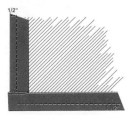

Diagram 6

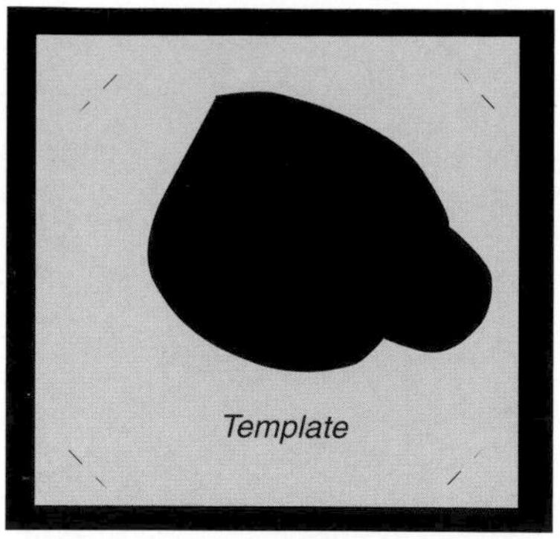

Diagram 1

Teacup Coaster

Materials needed for each coaster:

Scraps of cotton fabric in these colors: gold, dark blue, light gray, orange, and dark brown

Large scrap of fabric in contrasting color for binding; matching thread

6" x 6" piece of black felt

White embroidery floss

Scraps of fusible web

Tracing paper; pencil

Diagram 2

Make the Teacup Design

1. Using the pattern on page 11, trace the edges of the teacup and the outside edges of the design onto tracing paper. Cut out the teacup shape, leaving the rest of the paper intact. Place the template over the felt, with the outside edges parallel to the edges of the felt (Diagram 1).

2. Make the pattern overlay; see Basic Instructions. Use the overlay to trace all the pattern pieces onto fusible web. Pin the overlay to the felt and leave in place throughout the appliqué process.

3. Cut out the fabric pieces for the orange teacup, working with just a few pieces at a time. Peel off the paper backing and place on the felt, fusible side down, using the template as a guide to placement. Fuse the pieces. Repeat to complete the teacup (Diagram 2). Remove the template.

4. Cut out and fuse the gold saucer, then the dark brown tea (Diagram 3).

5. Cut out and fuse the dark blue background and the light gray corner pieces.

Diagram 3

Embroider the Details

Using 2 strands of white floss, stem-stitch the heat lines rising from the tea (Diagram 4).

Bind the Edges

Refer to Sunflower Coaster instructions on page 9.

Diagram 4

TEACUP COASTER Pattern

Gold

Dark Blue

Light Gray

Orange

Dark Brown

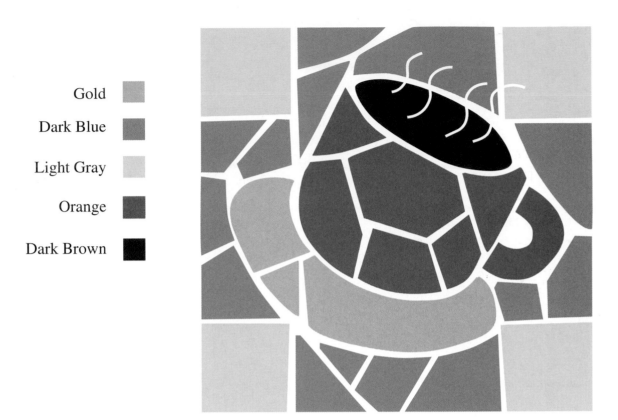

SUNFLOWER COASTER Pattern

Gold

Purple

Light Blue

Green

Framed Blue Vase

Materials:

Scraps of cotton fabric in these colors: pink, tan, rust, red, gold, dark gold, lavender print, purple, blue print, light green, green, and cream print

14" x 22" piece of dark green felt

Embroidery floss in these colors: black, red, gold, dark green, bright blue, and light blue

$3/8$ yard of fusible web

2 dark blue buttons, $3/8$"-diameter

Tracing paper; pencil

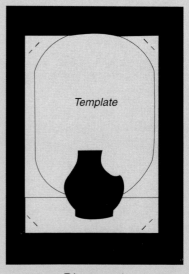

Template

Diagram 1

Make the Floral Design

1. Using the pattern on pages 15 and 16, make the pattern overlay; see Basic Instructions. You may need to tape together pieces of tracing paper to make a piece large enough. Note that the dashed lines on the pattern indicate where the 2 pages overlap.

2. Tape together another set of tracing papers. Working from the pattern overlay, trace the vase, the oval background, and the outside edges of the design onto tracing paper. Cut out inside the vase, leaving the rest of the paper intact. Place the template over the felt, with the outside edges parallel to the edges of the felt (Diagram 1).

3. Use the pattern overlay to trace all the pattern pieces onto fusible web. Pin the overlay to the felt and leave in place throughout the appliqué process.

4. Cut out the blue print vase, working with just a few pieces at a time. Peel off the paper backing and place on the felt, fusible side down, using the template as a guide to placement. Fuse the pieces (Diagram 2.)

5. Cut out inside the oval background on the template, leaving the rest of the paper intact. Place the template over the felt, aligning the same as before.

6. Cut out and fuse the red flower, leaving space for the embroidered center. Cut out and fuse the cream print/dark gold flower, then the gold/dark gold flower (Diagram 3).

7. Cut out and fuse the purple flowers. Cut out and fuse the light green leaves, then the light green stems and buds.

8. Cut out and fuse the pink flower. Cut out and fuse the lavender print background pieces, using the edge of the template to guide your placement. Remove the template (Diagram 4).

9. Cut out and fuse the green corner pieces. Cut out and fuse the tan pieces, then the rust pieces at the base of the vase.

Diagram 2

Diagram 3

Diagram 4

13

Embroider the Details

1. Following the pattern, satin-stitch the red flower center, using 2 strands of red floss.
2. Using 2 strands of gold floss, satin-stitch the centers of both buds at the top of the design. Make French knots in the dark gold center of the gold and cream print flowers, using 2 strands of floss wrapped once around the needle; see photo on page 12.
3. Satin-stitch the centers of the left bud, using 2 strands of bright blue floss.
4. Using 2 strands of dark green floss, buttonhole-stitch around the edges of the light green leaves. Sew a running stitch through the leaf centers; see photo on page 12.
5. Backstitch with 2 strands of light blue floss on selected petals of the purple flowers; see photo on page 12.
6. Using 2 strands of black floss, buttonhole-stitch around the outside edges of the petals on the red flower. Outline-stitch around the red satin stitching in the center. Make 3 French knots in the center of both round purple petals, using 2 strands of floss wrapped once around the needle; see photo on page 12.
7. Using 2 strands of black floss, buttonhole-stitch around the inside edges of the gold petals; see photo on page 12. Make small tack stitches around the outside edges. Repeat the buttonhole stitches and tack stitches on the cream print flower.

Complete the Design

1. Sew dark blue buttons to the green top corner pieces, using black floss.
2. Have the design framed professionally in a frame with a 10½" x 14½" opening.

Pink		Red		Lavender Print		Light Green	
Tan		Gold		Purple		Green	
Rust		Dark Gold		Blue Print		Cream Print	

Framed Summer Bouquet

Materials:

Scraps of cotton fabric in these colors: pink, purple, light green, green print,
  dark green, turquoise, light blue, medium blue, blue/black print, yellow,
  light gold, gold, orange, red, and rust/black print
22" x 24" piece of cream felt
Embroidery floss in these colors: black, rust, purple, turquoise, bright green, rose, and gold
1/2 yard of fusible web
Tracing paper; pencil

Make the Floral Design

1. Using the pattern on pages 20 through 22, make 1 pattern overlay for the vase, bouquet, and
background, including the band of stripes across the bottom; see Basic Instructions. You may
need to tape together pieces of tracing paper to make a piece large enough. Note that the
dashed lines on the pattern indicate where the pages overlap. Make a separate pattern overlay
for the top red center flower and the bottom blue center flower with a quarter of the border.

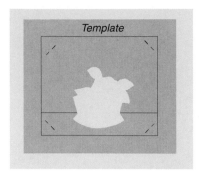

Diagram 1

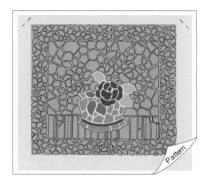

Diagram 2

Diagram 3

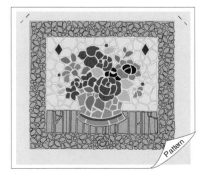

Diagram 4

2. Tape together another set of tracing papers. Working from the pattern overlay, trace the edges of the vase and large orange flower (including the leaves), the outside edges of the yellow background, and the outside edges of the blue/black print design onto tracing paper. Cut out inside the vase, flower, and leaves, leaving the rest of the paper intact. Place the template over the felt, with the outside edges parallel to the edges of the felt (Diagram 1).

3. Use the pattern overlay to trace all the pattern pieces onto fusible web. Note the light gold pieces (shown by yellow dashed lines) in the band across the bottom tuck under the blue/black print pieces. Pin the overlay to the felt and leave in place throughout the appliqué process.

4. Cut out the light blue fabric pieces for the bottom row of the vase, working with just a few pieces at a time. Peel off the paper backing and place on the felt, fusible side down, using the template as a guide to placement. Fuse the pieces. Cut out the turquoise band. The band should touch the light blue pieces of the bottom row. Fuse. Repeat to complete the vase.

5. Cut out and fuse the large orange flower, leaving space for the embroidered center. Cut out and fuse the green print leaves within the vase and the light green leaves near the orange flower (Diagram 2).

6. Cut out inside the yellow background on the template, leaving the rest of the paper intact. Place the template over the felt, aligning the same as before.

7. Cut out and fuse the red flower, leaving space for the embroidered center. Cut out and fuse the medium gold and rust/black print flower. Cut out and fuse 3 purple flowers, then 2 orange flowers (Diagram 3).

8. Cut out and fuse the remaining light green leaves and the light green bud. Cut out and fuse the pink flowers. Cut out and fuse the remaining green print leaves, the green print bud, and 3 small purple dots.

Make the Background

1. Cut out and fuse 2 blue/black print diamonds in the background. Cut out and fuse the yellow background pieces, using the edge of the template to guide your placement and following the number sequence (Diagram 4).

2. Cut out inside the blue/black print design on the template. Place the template over the felt, aligning the same as before.

3. Cut out and fuse the light gold pieces, using the edge of the template to guide your placement. Cut out and fuse the blue/black print pieces, overlapping the light gold pieces. Remove the template.

Make the Border

1. Mark the center of the bottom and top edges of the design. Cut out and fuse the top red center flower. Cut out and fuse the bottom medium blue center flower.

2. Working from the bottom blue center flower, cut out and fuse the bottom left quarter of the border design (Diagram 5). Cut out and fuse the top right, then top left and bottom right quarters of the border design, turning the pattern to fit as you go.

Embroider the Details

1. Using 2 strands of rust floss, satin-stitch the centers of the orange and red flowers. Buttonhole-stitch the outside edges of selected petals; see photo on page 17.

2. Make small tack stitches around the edges of the purple flower petals, using 2 strands of purple floss.

3. Using 2 strands of bright green floss, buttonhole-stitch the edges of the light green leaves next to the large orange flower. Outline-stitch the veins in the leaf centers. Make small tack stitches around the edges of the remaining light green and green print leaves, except for the light green bud and 2 left leaves; see photo on page 17. Couch the stems of the left pink flower and 2 green print leaves.

4. Using 2 strands of rose floss, satin-stitch the inside edges of the pink petals. Make small tack stitches around the outer edges.

5. Using 2 strands of gold floss, outline-stitch on the center petal of the top purple flower; see photo on page 17. Make French knots in each purple flower, wrapping the floss once around the needle. Make French knots on the rust/black print center of the gold flower. Make French knots in each red berry in the border, varying placement.

6. Using 2 strands of black floss, outline-stitch the left pink flower and 1 purple flower. Buttonhole-stitch the inside edge of the gold petals. Sew a black running stitch around the large orange flower and the outside of floral design; see photo on page 17. Sew a running stitch inside the floral border.

7. Using 2 strands of turquoise floss, buttonhole-stitch around the outside edges of the blue vase. Cross-stitch over the turquoise band with turquoise floss. Couch the centers of each cross stitch, using 2 strands of black floss.

Frame the Design

Have the design framed professionally in a frame with a 17" x 15" opening.

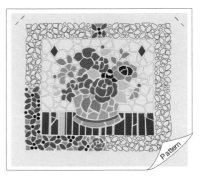

Diagram 5

FRAMED SUMMER BOUQUET Pattern

Bottom blue center flower

Basket Band

Turn border 90°
and repeat

FRAMED SUMMER BOUQUET Pattern

Top red
center flower

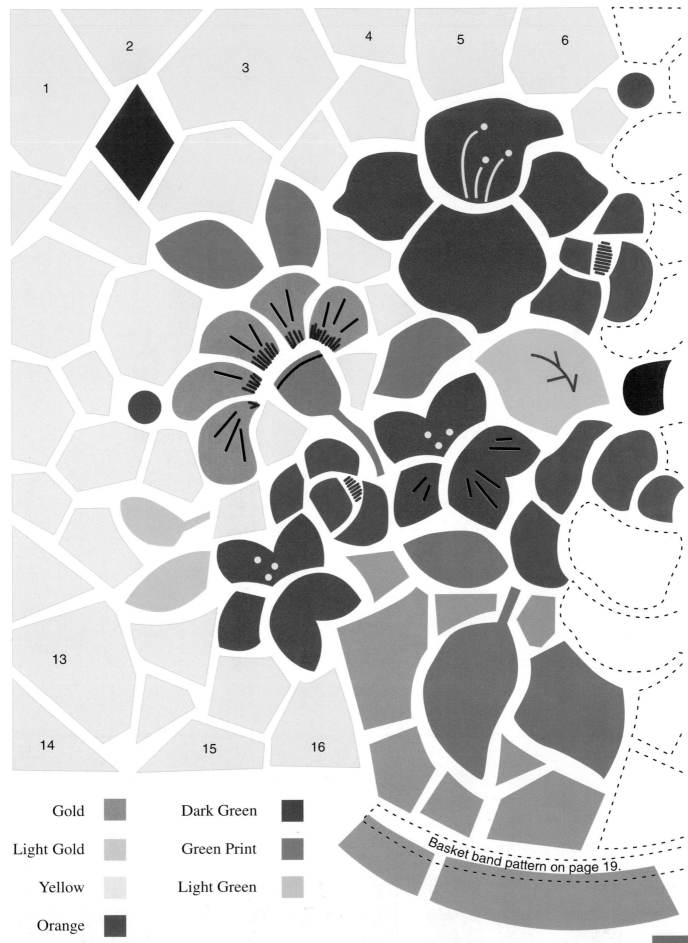

1

2

3

4

5

6

13

14

15

16

Gold

Light Gold

Yellow

Orange

Dark Green

Green Print

Light Green

Basket band pattern on page 19.

FRAMED SUMMER BOQUET Pattern

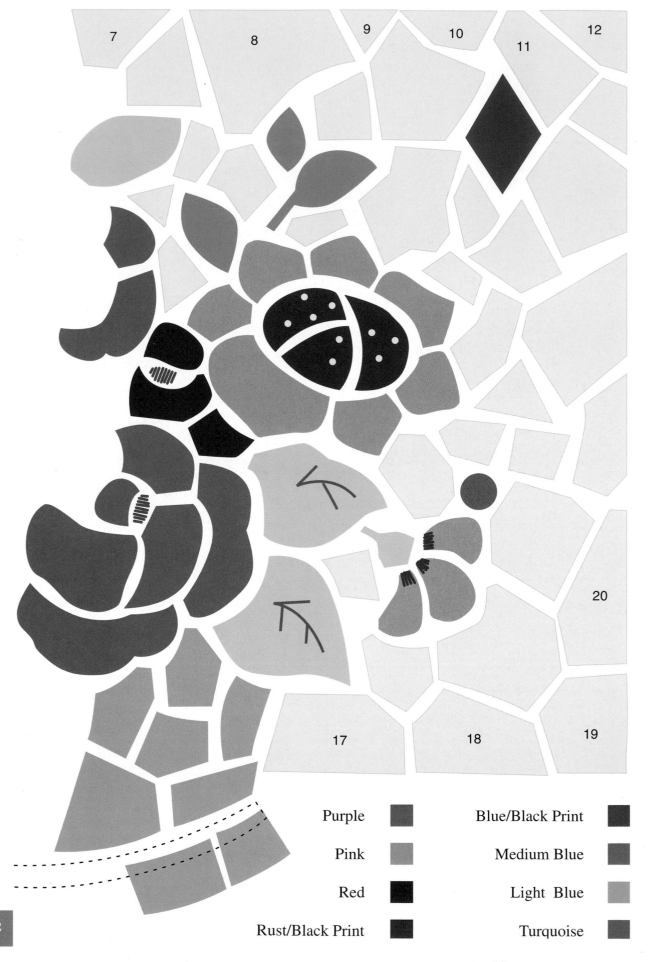

Purple		Blue/Black Print
Pink		Medium Blue
Red		Light Blue
Rust/Black Print		Turquoise

22

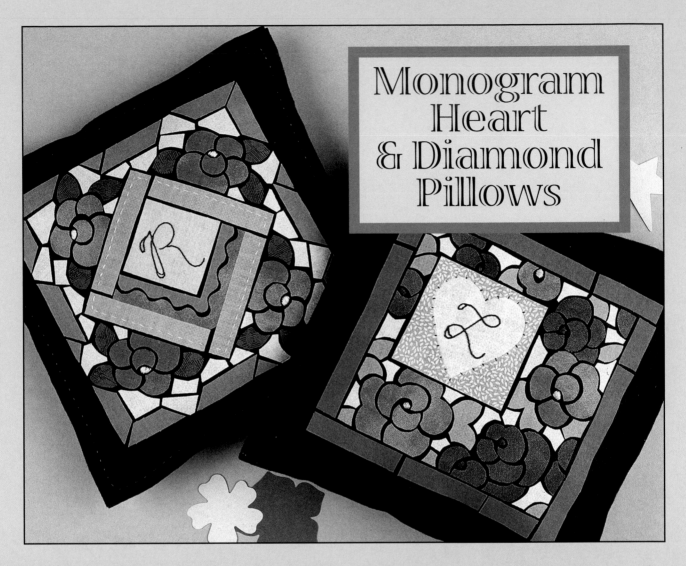

Monogram Heart & Diamond Pillows

Monogram Heart Pillow

Materials:

Scraps of cotton fabric in these colors: cream, lavender print, lavender, purple, green, and blue
2 squares of dark green felt, each 11" x 11"
Embroidery floss in these colors: dark green, purple, and lavender
$^1/_4$ yard of fusible web
Polyester stuffing
Tracing paper; pencil
Transfer pencil

Make the Floral Design

1. Using the pattern on page 25, trace the edges of the box around the heart, the outside edges of the floral design, and the outside edges of the square border onto tracing paper. Cut out the box around the heart, leaving the rest of the paper intact. Place the template over the felt, with the outside edges parallel to the edges of the felt (Diagram 1).

Diagram 1

Diagram 2

Diagram 3

Diagram 4

Diagram 5

2. Make the pattern overlay; see Basic Instructions. Use the overlay to trace all the pattern pieces onto fusible web. Pin the overlay to the felt and leave in place throughout the appliqué process.

3. Cut out the fabric piece for the heart, adding $\frac{1}{8}$" to all edges. Peel off the paper backing and place on the felt, fusible side down, using the pattern overlay as a guide. Cut out the lavender print box and place on top of the heart. Fuse the pieces (Diagram 2). Remove the template.

4. Using the pattern overlay as a guide, cut out and fuse 2 or 3 pieces for 1 flower, then the leaves. Cut out and fuse the remaining flowers and leaves (Diagram 3).

5. Cut out and fuse the cream background and blue border (Diagram 4).

Embroider the Details

1. Using the transfer pencil, transfer the desired monogram from page 28 to the heart, following the manufacturer's instructions; see Basic Instructions. Stem-stitch the monogram, using 2 strands of dark green floss.

2. Make small tack stitches around the heart, using 1 strand of dark green floss and stitching through all layers.

3. Satin-stitch the lavender flower centers, using 2 strands of lavender floss. Repeat for the purple flowers with purple floss.

Make the Pillow

1. Trim the felt pieces to $9\frac{1}{2}$" x $9\frac{1}{2}$", with the edges parallel to the edges of the design. Align the two pieces of felt. Sew a running stitch $\frac{1}{4}$" from the outside edges, using 2 strands of dark green floss. Leave the fourth edge open but do not cut the floss (Diagram 5).

2. Stuff the pillow moderately. Sew the pillow shut, continuing the running stitch on the fourth edge.

Lavender Print | Lavender | Purple | Cream | Green | Blue

Diagram 1

Diagram 2

Diagram 3

Diagram 4

Monogram Diamond Pillow

Materials:

Scraps of cotton fabric in these colors: gold, blue, cream, purple, turquoise, and green

2 squares of dark green felt, each 11" x 11"

Embroidery floss in these colors: navy and cream

¼ yard of fusible web

Polyester stuffing

Transfer pencil

Tracing paper; drawing pencil

Make the Floral Design

1. Using the pattern on page 27, trace the edges of the diamond border and the outside edges of the border onto tracing paper. Cut out the diamond, leaving the rest of the paper intact. Place the template over the felt, with the outside edges parallel to the edges of the felt (Diagram 1).

2. Make the pattern overlay; see Basic Instructions. Trace all the pattern pieces onto fusible web. Pin the overlay to the felt and leave in place throughout the appliqué process.

3. Cut out the fabric for the gold diamond. Peel off the paper backing and place on the felt, fusible side down, using the pattern overlay as a guide. Fuse. Cut out the blue and purple pieces, adding ⅛" to the straight edges of the purple piece. Fuse. Cut out and fuse the turquoise pieces, overlapping the purple pieces (Diagram 2). Remove the template.

4. Using the pattern overlay as a guide, cut out and fuse 2 or 3 pieces for 1 flower, then the leaves. Cut out and fuse the remaining flowers and leaves (Diagram 3).

5. Cut out and fuse the cream background and blue border (Diagram 4).

Embroider the Details

1. Using the transfer pencil, transfer the desired monogram from page 28 to the diamond, following the manufacturer's instructions; see Basic Instructions. Stem-stitch the monogram, using 2 strands of navy floss.

2. Satin-stitch the purple flower centers, using 2 strands of cream floss. Sew a running stitch ⅛" from the outside edge of the turquoise border, using cream floss.

Make the Pillow

Refer to Monogram Heart Pillow instructions on page 24.

MONOGRAM DIAMOND PILLOW Pattern

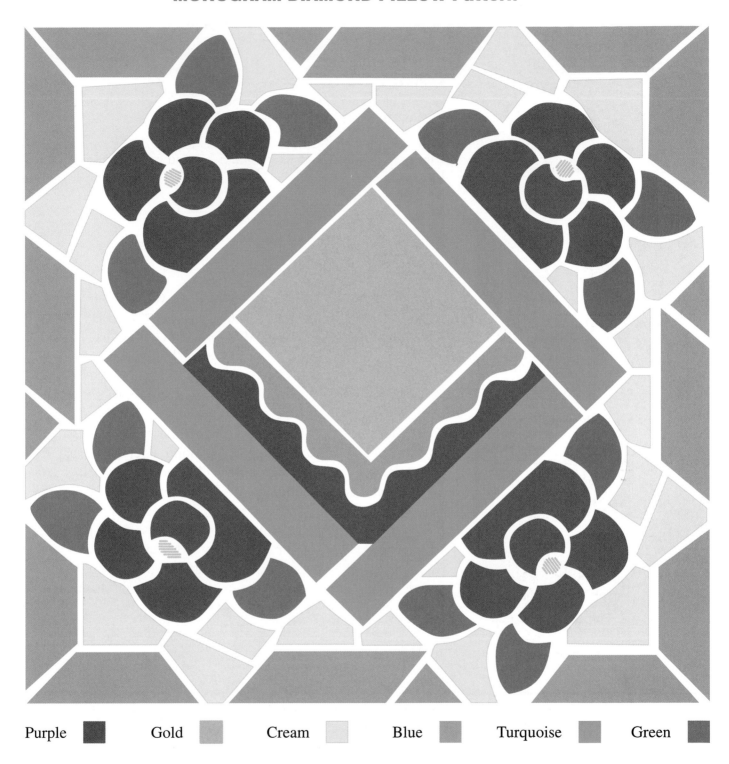

Purple ▦   Gold ▦   Cream ▦   Blue ▦   Turquoise ▦   Green ▦

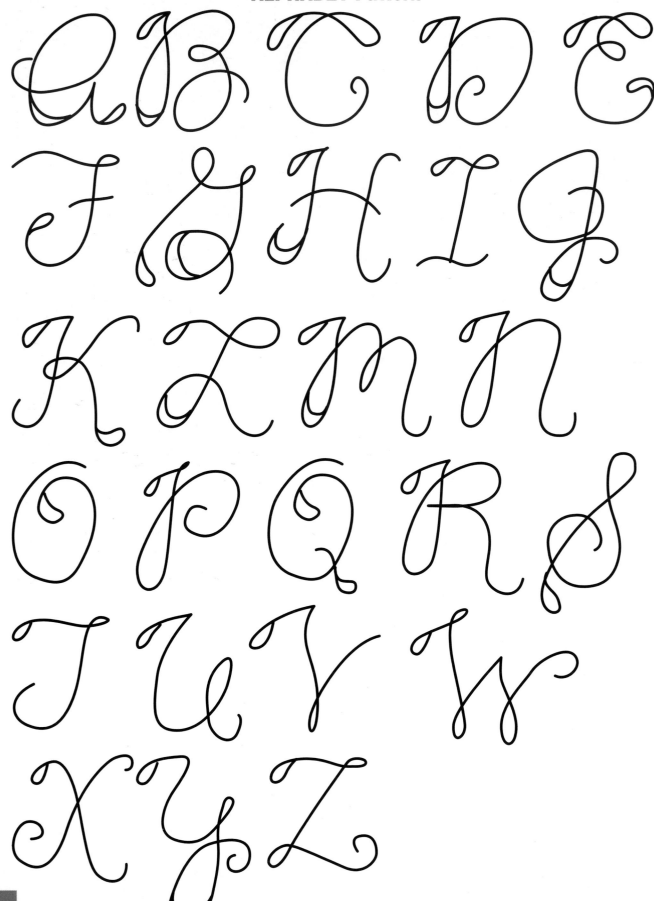

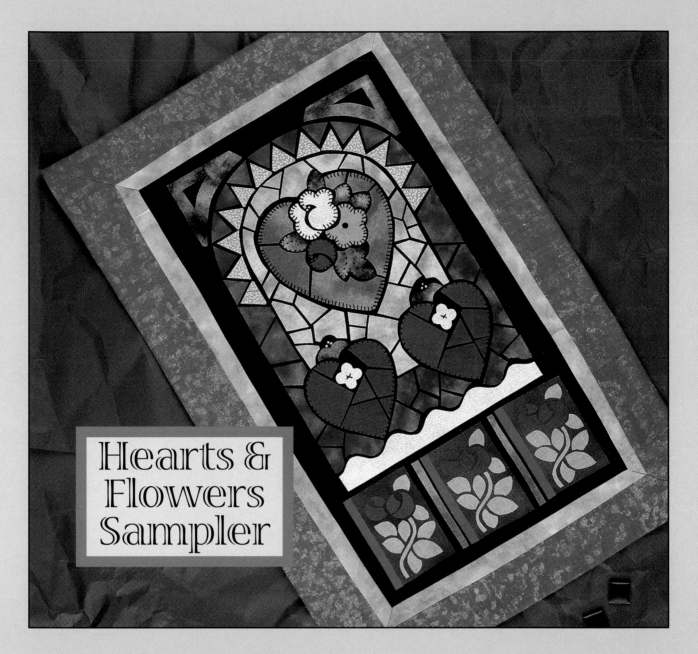

Hearts & Flowers Sampler

Materials:

Scraps of cotton fabric in these colors: light purple, purple, dark purple, gold, cream print, dark rust, orange, medium blue, light gray, green, aqua, and turquoise

$^1/_4$ yard of gold fabric

$^3/_8$ yard of navy blue fabric

$^1/_2$ yard of turquoise fabric

Embroidery floss in these colors: black, green, and yellow

$^3/_8$ yard of fusible web

$^1/_2$ yard of polyester fleece

$^1/_4$"-diameter dowel, $15^1/_2$" long

Tracing paper; pencil

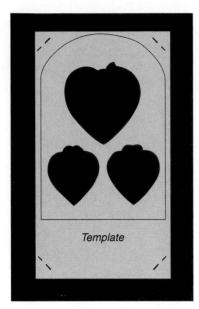

Diagram 1

Make the Floral Design

1. Cut a 12" x 19" piece of navy blue fabric for the background of the design.

2. Using the pattern on pages 32, 33, and 34, make 1 pattern overlay for the floral design, including the band of 3 floral motifs ¼" below the arched floral design; see Basic Instructions. You may need to tape together pieces of tracing paper to make a piece large enough.

3. Tape together another set of tracing papers. Working from the pattern overlay, trace the edges of the 3 hearts, including the flowers that extend from the tops. Also trace the outside edge of the arch. Cut out the hearts and flowers, leaving the rest of the paper intact. Place the template on the background, with the outside edges parallel to the edges of the fabric (Diagram 1).

4. Use the pattern overlay to trace all the pattern pieces onto fusible web. Note that the turquoise pieces between the floral motifs slightly overlap the purple backgrounds. Pin the overlay to the navy background and leave in place throughout the appliqué process.

5. Cut out the cream print flowers, working with just a few pieces at a time. Peel off the paper backing and place on the background, fusible side down, using the pattern overlay as a guide. Fuse the pieces. Cut out and fuse the remaining flowers inside the hearts, then the leaves (Diagram 2).

6. Cut out the arch on the template, leaving the rest of the paper intact.

7. Cut out and fuse the light gray background. Cut out and fuse the light purple points in the top of the arch, then the medium blue arch and background. Cut out and fuse the cream print border (Diagram 3). Remove the template.

8. Cut out and fuse the green corner pieces.

9. Assemble the 3 floral motifs. Cut out 3 dark purple 3" x 4½" pieces of fabric without fusible web. On each piece, cut out and fuse the orange flower, then the stem and leaves. Attach fusible web to the purple pieces. Trim the dark purple pieces to 2¼" x 3⅝", with the top, bottom, and right edges of the design ⅛" from the cut edges of the dark purple fabric; the left edge of the design will be ¼" from the left edge of the fabric. Note that these distances are not apparent on the pattern.

10. Fuse the 3 floral motifs to the background, using the pattern overlay as a guide. Cut out and fuse 3 turquoise strips to the left edges of the dark purple pieces. The pieces should overlap slightly. Cut out and fuse 2 purple strips between the floral motifs (Diagram 4).

Diagram 2

Embroider the Details

1. Using 2 strands of black floss, buttonhole-stitch the edges of the cream print and gold flowers and the purple heart. Satin-stitch the gold flower center. Make small tack stitches on the edges of the orange flower, the leaves in the purple heart, and the edges of the rust hearts. Sew a running stitch for the veins in 3 leaves; see photo on page 29. Make 1 large cross stitch in the center of the cream motif in the rust hearts.
2. Make 3 French knots in the cream flower and above the motifs with rust hearts, using 2 strands of yellow floss wrapped once around the needle. Make 3 green French knots in the rust flower in the purple heart.

Complete the Wall Hanging

1. Trim the navy background to 10¼" x 18", with the bottom, left, and right edges of the dark purple motifs the same distance from the edges of the navy fabric. From turquoise fabric, cut the following: 1 piece, 16" x 24"; 2 pieces, 4½" x 17"; and 2 pieces, 4½" x 25". From the gold fabric, cut the following: 2 pieces, 1⅛" x 17"; and 2 pieces, 1⅛" x 25".
2. Match 1 gold piece to each 4½"-wide turquoise piece. Stitch with right sides together on 1 long edge. Press.
3. Mark the center of each edge of the navy background. Also mark the center of the long edge of each gold piece. Match the center of 1 gold strip to the top edge of the navy background; pin. Using a ¼" seam, stitch the gold edge of the gold/turquoise strip to the navy background, stopping ¼" from each edge of the navy piece (Diagram 5). The gold strips will be ⅝" wide. Repeat with each edge and the remaining gold/turquoise strips. Do not allow the stitching to extend into the ¼" seam allowances.
4. To miter the corners, fold the right sides of adjacent gold/turquoise strips together and stitch at a 45-degree angle (Diagram 6). Trim the seam allowance to ¼" and press. Repeat for each corner. The finished design piece will be 15½" x 23¼".
5. Cut 1 piece of polyester fleece 15½" x 22¾". Center on the back of the design piece. Pin securely. Center the right side of the design piece over the right side of the turquoise backing piece. Using a ¼" seam, stitch the edges of the front and back together, leaving an opening in the bottom edge. Trim the seam allowance on all edges to ¼". Trim the fleece from the seam allowances. Trim the corners. Turn. Slipstitch the opening closed. Whipstitch the dowel to the top back edge of the wall hanging.

Diagram 3

Diagram 4

Diagram 5

Diagram 6

Orange

Aqua

Dark Purple

Turquoise

Light Purple

Gold

Dark Rust

Purple

Cream Print

Medium Blue

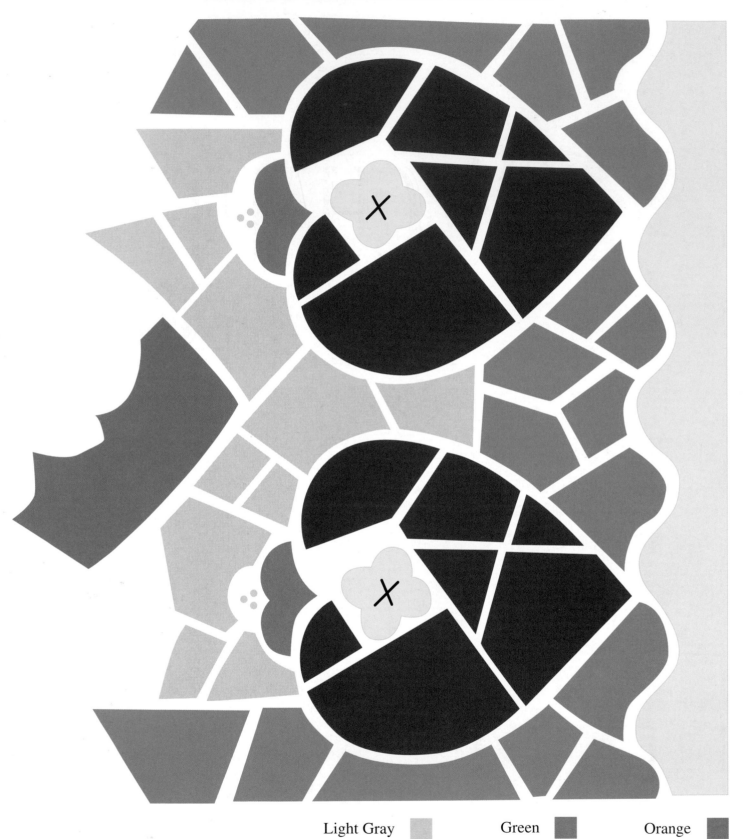

Light Gray   Green   Orange

CHAPTER TWO

KIND WORDS ARE LIKE HONEY

Sheep Wall Hanging

Materials:

Scraps of cotton fabric in these colors: cream print, light gold,
     tan print, brown, light turquoise, dark turquoise, and pale gray
³/₄ yard of brown print fabric; matching thread
17" x 15" piece of black felt
Black embroidery floss
¹/₄ yard of fusible web
5 assorted buttons; white thread
¹/₄"-diameter dowel, 14¹/₂" long
Tracing paper; pencil

Make the Sheep Design

1. Using the pattern on pages 38 and 39, make 1 pattern overlay for the sheep; see Basic
Instructions. You may need to tape together pieces of tracing paper to make a piece large
enough. Note that the dashed lines on the pattern indicate where the 2 pages overlap.

Make a separate pattern overlay for the grass, joining the 2 pieces of the grass pattern into 1. Use the overlay to trace all the pattern pieces onto fusible web. Pin the overlay to the felt and leave in place throughout the appliqué process.

2. Tape together another set of tracing papers larger than the design. Working from the pattern overlay, trace the edges of the sheep and the outside edge of the design onto tracing paper. Cut out the sheep, leaving the rest of the paper intact. Place the template over the felt, with the outside edges parallel to the edges of the felt (Diagram 1).

3. Cut out fabric pieces for the sheep's head, working with just a few pieces at a time. Peel off the paper backing and place on the felt, fusible side down, using the template as a guide to placement. Fuse the pieces. Repeat to complete the sheep's head.

4. Cut out and fuse the sheep's legs, then the fleece (Diagram 2). Remove the template. Cut out and fuse the grass, then the background (Diagram 3).

Embroider the Details

Using black floss, satin-stitch the sheep's eyes. Make large buttonhole stitches on the outside edges of the sheep's horns; see photo on page 36.

Finish the Wall Hanging

1. Trim the felt to 15" x 13½", with the top and side edges of the design 1½" from the edges of the felt and the bottom edge of the design 2¾" from the edge.

2. Cut 1 piece of the brown print fabric 19½" x 19". Place the felt on the wrong side of the fabric, with the top and side edges of the felt 3½" from the fabric edge. Pin securely.

3. Turn under the top raw edge, then fold the fabric down over the felt to within ⅛" of the design, allowing 1½" of the fabric to show. Slipstitch. Repeat with both sides, allowing 1½" of the fabric to show on the front. Turn up the bottom edge and slipstitch, allowing 2¾" of the fabric to show.

4. Sew the buttons on the left edge of the design.

5. To make a hanging sleeve, cut a 14" x 1½" strip of plaid fabric. Fold the short raw edges under twice and hem. Fold the strip in half lengthwise, right sides together. Stitch a ¼" seam along the long edge. Turn right side out. Slipstitch the sleeve to the top edge of the wall hanging back. Insert the dowel. Tack the bottom edge to the wall hanging back.

Diagram 1

Diagram 2

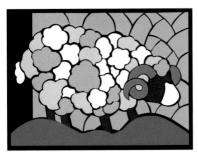

Diagram 3

Light Turquoise

Dark Turquoise

Pale Gray

Cream Print

Light Gold

Tan Print

Brown

Beehive Wall Hanging

Materials:

Scraps of cotton fabric in these colors: light gold, gold, dark gold, tan, brown, light green, green, purple, light blue, dark blue, and white

⅝ yard of green fabric; matching thread

15½" x 17" piece of black felt

Embroidery floss in these colors: black, bright green, and golden brown

¼ yard of fusible web

¼"-diameter dowel, 15" long

Dressmaker's chalk

Tracing paper; pencil

Transfer pencil

Make the Beehive

1. Using the pattern on pages 43 and 44, make 1 pattern overlay for the beehive and gold border; see Basic Instructions. You may need to tape together pieces of tracing paper to make a piece large enough. Note that the dashed lines on the pattern indicate where the 2 pages overlap.

2. Tape together another set of tracing papers. Working from the pattern overlay, trace the beehive and inside edges of the gold border onto tracing paper. Cut out inside the beehive and around the outside edge, leaving the rest of the paper intact.

3. Using chalk, mark a square on the felt that is 3¹/₄" from the top, right, and left edges, and 5" from the bottom edge of the felt. Center the template in the square (Diagram 1).

4. Use the pattern overlay to trace all the pattern pieces onto fusible web. Pin the overlay to the felt, matching the edges of the gold border, and leave in place throughout the appliqué process.

5. Cut out the bottom row of the beehive, working with just a few pieces at a time. Peel off the paper backing and place on the felt, fusible side down, using the template as a guide to placement. Fuse. Cut out and fuse the brown door (Diagram 2).

6. Continue to cut out and fuse beehive pieces. Cut out and fuse the bee on the hive. Remove the template.

7. Cut out and fuse the 3 purple flowers that touch the beehive (Diagram 3).

8. Cut out and fuse the pieces in the grass below the beehive, using the chalk line as a guide and keeping the lower edges parallel to the chalk line.

9. Cut out and fuse the purple flowers, clouds, and sky on the left side of the beehive. Repeat the process on the right side of the beehive. Use the chalk line as a guide and keep the outside edges parallel to the chalk line (Diagram 4).

Make the Border

1. Trace the outside edges of 1 corner bee motif onto tracing paper. Cut out the template. Place the corner template over the felt (Diagram 4).

2. Cut out and fuse 1 corner bee motif. Rotate the block and repeat for each corner; see photo on page 40.

3. Cut out and fuse the dark gold strips. Cut out and fuse the purple and green checkerboard.

Diagram 1

Diagram 2

Diagram 3

Diagram 4

Embroider the Details

1. Using 2 strands of black floss, buttonhole-stitch around the outside edges of the beehive, including the door. Also buttonhole-stitch the edges of the dark gold strips. Using 2 strands of floss wrapped once around the needle, make French knots at random in the grass. Make 3 closely grouped French knots in the smallest pieces of each purple flower. To make antennae for the bee, make 2 long stitches above the bee's head over the nearest contrasting fabric. Make 1 French knot at the end of each antenna, using 2 strands of floss wrapped once around the needle. Repeat for the bees in the corners. Satin-stitch the stripes on the backs of the bees.

2. Backstitch the outline for the wings, using 1 strand of black floss.

3. Satin-stitch the 2-part leaves, using 2 strands of green floss. It may be helpful to use dressmaker's chalk to draw the leaf shape on the felt.

Finish the Wall Hanging

1. Cut 1 piece of green fabric 19$\frac{1}{2}$" x 22$\frac{3}{4}$" for the backing. Place the green fabric, wrong side up, on a flat surface. Place the felt over the green fabric, with the edges parallel, allowing 2" on the top, left, and right, and 3$\frac{3}{4}$" on the bottom. Pin the felt to the background.

2. Sew a running stitch outside the border through the felt and background.

3. Turn under the top raw edge, then fold the fabric over the felt to within $\frac{1}{8}$" of the design. Slipstitch the folded edge with green thread. Repeat the process on the left and right sides, lapping the left and right sides over the top at the corners.

4. Turn under the raw edge, then fold the bottom edge up over the felt; slipstitch the folded edge, lapping the bottom over the left and right sides at the corners.

5. Trace the saying onto tracing paper. Following the manufacturer's instructions, use a transfer pencil or artist's transfer paper to transfer the saying to the bottom section.

6. Stem-stitch the saying, using 1 strand of golden brown floss. Make French knots in the center of each O, using 1 strand of floss wrapped twice around the needle.

7. To make a hanging sleeve, cut a 15" x 1$\frac{1}{2}$" strip of green fabric. Fold the short raw edges under twice and hem. Fold the strip in half lengthwise, right sides together. Stitch a $\frac{1}{4}$" seam along the long edge. Turn right side out. Slipstitch the sleeve to the top edge of the wall hanging back. Insert the dowel. Tack the bottom edge to the wall hanging back.

Gold Border   Cut 4

Light Gold

Gold

Dark Gold

Tan

Brown

Light Green

BEEHIVE WALL HANGING
Pattern

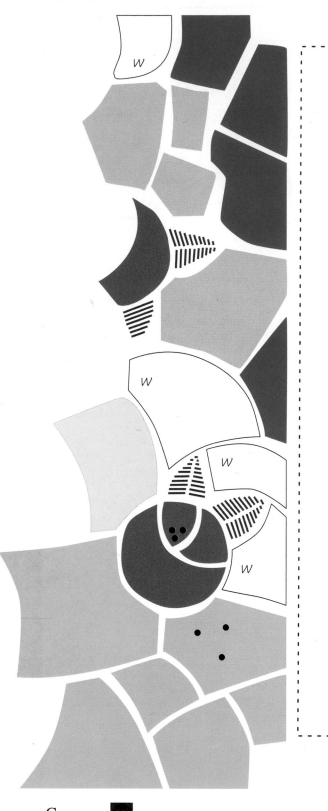

Green	⬛	
Purple	⬛	Dark Blue ⬛
Light Blue	⬛	White [w]

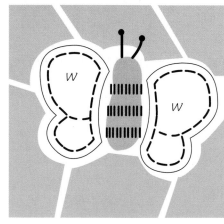

Spotted Cow
Wall Hanging

Materials:

Scraps of cotton fabric in these colors: white, cream print, tan, cream, light brown, rust, blue, and blue-green

$3/4$ yard of blue/navy woven plaid fabric; matching thread

17" x 15" piece of black felt

Embroidery floss in these colors: black and gray

$1/4$ yard of fusible web

2 tan buttons, $5/8$"-diameter

1 white button, $7/8$"-diameter

$1/4$"-diameter dowel, 14" long

Tracing paper; pencil

Diagram 1

Diagram 2

Diagram 3

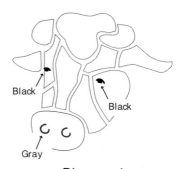

Black

Black

Gray

Diagram 4

Make the Cow Design

1. Using the pattern on pages 47 and 48, make 1 pattern overlay for the cow; see Basic Instructions. You may need to tape together pieces of tracing paper to make a piece large enough. Note that the dashed lines on the pattern indicate where the 2 pages overlap. Make a separate pattern overlay for the grass, joining the 2 pieces of the grass pattern into 1. Use the overlay to trace all the pattern pieces onto fusible web. Pin the overlay to the felt and leave in place throughout the appliqué process.

2. Tape together another set of tracing papers larger than the design. Working from the pattern overlay, trace the edges of the cow and the outside edge of the design onto tracing paper. Cut out the cow, leaving the rest of the paper intact. Place the template over the felt, with the outside edges parallel to the edges of the felt (Diagram 1).

3. Cut out the fabric pieces for the cow's head (except the snout), working with just a few pieces at a time. Peel off the paper backing and place on the felt, fusible side down, using the template as a guide to placement. Fuse the pieces. Repeat to complete the cow's head.

4. Cut out and fuse the cow's legs, then the white area. Cut out and fuse the cow's spots (Diagram 2). Remove the template.

5. Cut out and fuse the grass, then the background. Cut out and fuse the cow's snout (Diagram 3).

Embroider the Details

1. Satin-stitch the cow's eyes, using 2 strands of black floss (Diagram 4).

2. Backstitch the cow's nostril, using 2 strands of gray floss.

Finish the Wall Hanging

Refer to Sheep Wall Hanging instructions on page 37.

Blue   Blue-Green   White w   Cream Print

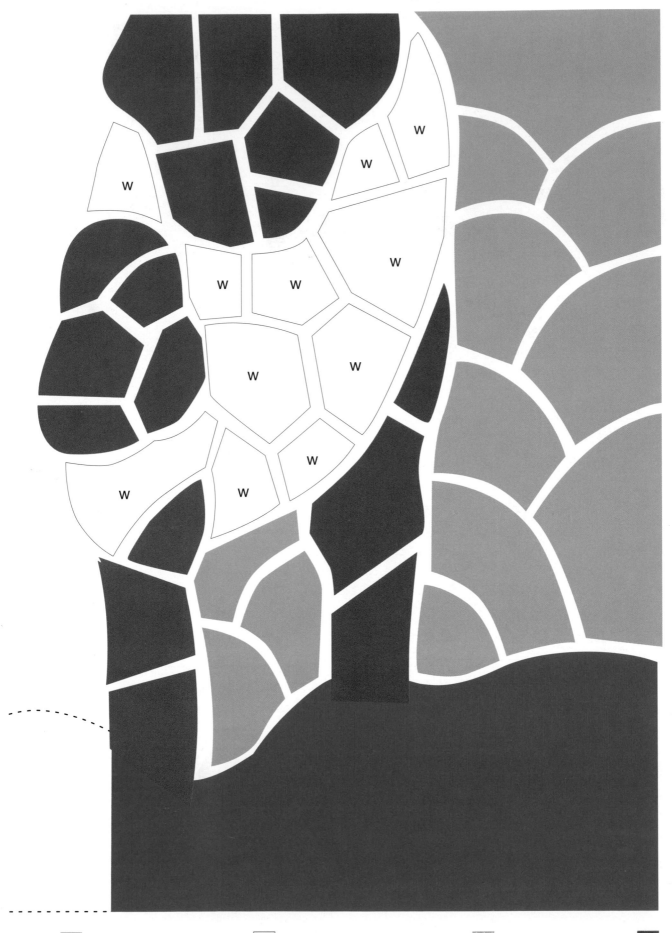

Tan   Cream   C   Light Brown   Rust

Butterfly, Floral, & Cat Gift Bags

Purple Butterfly Gift Bag

Materials:

Scraps of cotton fabric in these colors: brown, lavender, purple,
   blue, blue-green, gold, and orange
$5\frac{1}{2}$" x 23" piece of orange fabric; matching thread
5" x 5" piece of white felt; matching thread
Embroidery floss in these colors: black and purple
Scraps of fusible web
$\frac{1}{2}$ yard of $\frac{1}{8}$"-diameter navy blue cord
Embroidery scissors
Tracing paper; pencil
Transfer pencil

Make the Butterfly Design

1. Using the pattern on page 51, trace the edges of the butterfly and the outside edge of the design onto tracing paper. Cut out the butterfly, leaving the rest of the paper intact. Place the template

Diagram 1

Diagram 2

over the felt, with the outside edges parallel to the edges of the felt (Diagram 1).

2. Make the pattern overlay; see Basic Instructions. Use the overlay to trace all the pattern pieces onto fusible web. Pin the overlay to the felt and leave in place throughout the appliqué process.

3. Cut out the fabric piece for the butterfly body. Peel off the paper backing and place on the felt, fusible side down, using the template as a guide to placement. Fuse.

4. Cut out and fuse the blue and orange sections of the wings, then the gold and orange sections.

5. Cut out and fuse the lavender and purple sections. Cut and fuse the remainder of the wings (Diagram 2). Remove the template and the pattern overlay.

Complete the Felt Design

Following the manufacturer's instructions, use a transfer pencil to make the pattern for the openwork in the felt. Transfer it to the back of the felt, checking your work to be sure the openwork fits around the butterfly. Cut out the open spaces, using embroidery scissors. Don't worry if parts of the pattern lines still show on the back.

Embroider the Details

1. Using 2 strands of purple floss, buttonhole-stitch selected edges of the wings; see photo on page 49. Make French knots in the small pieces near the body, wrapping floss once around the needle. Satin-stitch spots on the orange and yellow sections.

2. Using 2 strands of black floss, stem-stitch the antennae. Make a French knot at the end of each, wrapping floss once around the needle.

Make the Gift Bag

1. Trim the felt to measure 4½" x 4½".

2. Fold the orange fabric, right side out, to measure 5½" x 11½". Place the felt piece ¼" above the fold and center it; pin to the top layer of fabric. Using thread to match the felt, slipstitch the felt to the fabric, sewing all the outside edges and the edges of the openwork.

3. Refold the orange fabric, right sides together. Stitch the long sides with a ¼" seam. Fold the top edge 1¾" to the wrong side; turn the raw edge under ¼" and hem the folded edge. Turn the bag right side out. Insert the gift and tie the cord around the bag.

Brown

Lavender

Purple

Blue

Blue-Green

Gold

Orange

Blue Butterfly Gift Bag

Materials:

Scraps of cotton fabric in these colors: light turquoise, medium
   turquoise, medium blue, gold, orange, brown, and black
5 ½" x 23" piece of orange fabric; matching thread
5" x 5" piece of white felt; matching thread
Embroidery floss in these colors: purple, gold, and black
Scraps of fusible web
½ yard of ⅛"-diameter navy blue cord
Embroidery scissors
Tracing paper; pencil
Transfer pencil

Make the Butterfly Design

1. Using the pattern on page 52, trace the edges of the butterfly
   and the outside edge of the design onto tracing paper. Cut out
   the butterfly, leaving the rest of the paper intact. Place the
   template over the felt, with the outside edges parallel to the
   edges of the felt (Diagram 1).

Template

Diagram 1

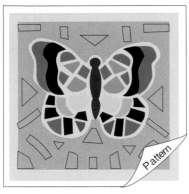

Diagram 2

2. Make the pattern overlay; see Basic Instructions. Use the overlay to trace all the pattern pieces onto fusible web. Pin the overlay to the felt and leave in place throughout the appliqué process.

3. Cut out the fabric piece for the butterfly body. Peel off the paper backing and place on the felt, fusible side down, using the template as a guide to placement. Fuse.

4. Cut out and fuse the blue and orange sections of the wings, then the black and orange sections. The pieces should touch.

5. Cut out and fuse the light turquoise sections. Cut and fuse the remainder of the wings (Diagram 2). Remove the template and the pattern overlay.

Complete the Felt Design

Refer to Purple Butterfly Gift Bag instructions on page 50.

Embroider the Details

1. Using 2 strands of purple floss, buttonhole-stitch around the edges of the upper orange sections. Also buttonhole-stitch around the light turquoise pieces; see photo on page 49. Make French knots in the small orange pieces of the upper wing, wrapping floss once around the needle. Sew a running stitch through the center of the gold pieces in the lower wings.

**BLUE BUTTERFLY
GIFT BAG Pattern**

Light Turquoise

Medium Turquoise

Medium Blue

Gold

Orange

Brown

Black

2. Using 2 strands of gold floss, buttonhole-stitch around the outside of the lower wing pieces. Make V-shaped long stitches in the black sections of the upper wings.

3. Using 2 strands of black floss, stem-stitch the antennae. Make a French knot at the end of each, wrapping floss once around the needle.

Make the Gift Bag

Refer to Purple Butterfly Gift Bag instructions on page 50.

Floral Gift Bag

Materials:

Scraps of cotton fabric in these colors: lavender print, green, and medium blue
5½" x 23" piece of blue print fabric; matching thread
5" x 5" piece of white felt; matching thread
Embroidery floss in these colors: cream and turquoise
Scraps of fusible web
½ yard of ⅛"-diameter navy blue cord
Embroidery scissors
Tracing paper; pencil
Transfer pencil

Make the Floral Design

1. Using the pattern on page 54, trace the edges of the flower and the outside edge of the design onto tracing paper. Cut out the flower, leaving the rest of the paper intact. Place the template over the felt, with the outside edges parallel to the edges of the felt (Diagram 1).

2. Make the pattern overlay; see Basic Instructions. Use the overlay to trace all the pattern pieces onto fusible web. Pin the overlay to the felt and leave in place throughout the appliqué process.

3. Cut out fabric pieces for the flower, working with just a few pieces at a time. Peel off the paper backing and place on the felt, fusible side down, using the template as a guide to placement. Fuse the pieces (Diagram 2). Remove the template.

4. Cut out and fuse 1 group of leaves at a time. Cut out and fuse the lavender print background.

Complete the Felt Design

Refer to Purple Butterfly Gift Bag instructions on page 50.

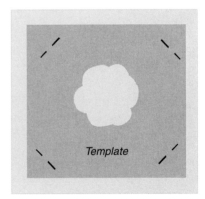

Diagram 1

Diagram 2

Embroider the Details

1. Using 2 strands of turquoise floss, sew a running stitch around the flower pieces.

2. Using 2 strands of cream floss, sew a long stitch in the center of each leaf. Make a French knot at the end of each long stitch, wrapping floss once around the needle.

Make the Gift Bag

Refer to Purple Butterfly Gift Bag instructions on page 50, using the blue print fabric.

FLORAL GIFT BAG
Pattern

Lavender Print

Green

Medium Blue

Cat Gift Bag

Materials:

Scraps of cotton fabric in these colors: light rust, medium rust, dark brown, rust print, light turquoise, and medium turquoise

$5^1/_2$" x 23" piece of blue print fabric; matching thread

5" x $6^1/_2$" piece of white felt; matching thread

Embroidery floss in these colors: black, brown, purple, and tan

Scraps of fusible web

$^1/_2$ yard of $^1/_8$"-diameter navy blue cord

Embroidery scissors

Tracing paper; pencil

Transfer pencil

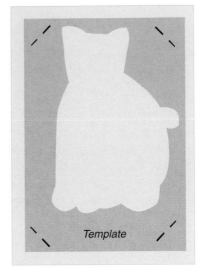

Diagram 1

Make the Cat Design

1. Using the pattern on page 56, trace the edges of the cat and the outside edges of the design onto tracing paper. Cut out the cat, leaving the rest of the paper intact. Place the template over the felt, with the outside edges parallel to the edges of the felt (Diagram 1).

2. Make the pattern overlay; see Basic Instructions. Use the overlay to trace all the pattern pieces onto fusible web. Pin the overlay to the felt and leave in place throughout the appliqué process.

3. Cut out fabric pieces for the cat's head, working with just a few pieces at a time. Peel off the paper backing and place on the felt, fusible side down, using the template as a guide to placement. Fuse the pieces.

4. Cut out and fuse the cat's body (Diagram 2). Remove template.

5. Cut out and fuse the light turquoise and medium turquoise scalloped borders.

Diagram 2

Complete the Felt Design

Following the manufacturer's instructions, use a transfer pencil to make the pattern for the openwork in the felt. Transfer it to the back of the felt, checking your work to be sure the openwork fits around the cat. Cut out the open spaces, using embroidery scissors. Don't worry if parts of the pattern lines still show on the back.

Embroider the Details

1. Buttonhole-stitch selected edges of the cat's body, using 2 strands of brown floss; see photo on page 49.

2. Using 2 strands of black floss, make French knots for the eyes, wrapping floss once around the needle. Satin-stitch the nose. Backstitch the mouth.

3. Using 2 strands of tan floss, sew long stitches for the whiskers.

4. Make French knots in the center of each scallop, using 2 strands of purple floss and wrapping the floss once around the needle. Sew a running stitch below the scallops.

Make the Gift Bag

1. Trim the felt to measure 4" x 5³/₄".

2. Refer to Purple Butterfly Gift Bag instructions on page 50, using the blue print fabric.

**CAT GIFT BAG
Pattern**

Light Rust

Medium Rust

Rust Print

Dark Brown

Light Turquoise

Medium Turquoise

Framed Sunshine

Materials:

Scraps of cotton fabric in these colors: yellow, gold, dark gold, gold print, rose, dark blue, medium blue, light blue, dark rust, and purple

15" x 15" piece of black felt

Embroidery floss in these colors: black, royal blue, purple, turquoise, and gold

¼ yard of fusible web

2 pieces of polyester fleece, each 10" x 10"

Tracing paper; pencil

Make the Sun Design

1. Using the pattern on page 59, trace the edges of the circle around the face and the outside edges of the design onto tracing paper. Cut out inside the circle, leaving the rest of the

Template

Diagram 1

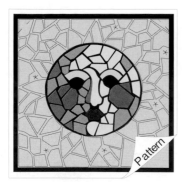

Diagram 2

Diagram 3

Diagram 4

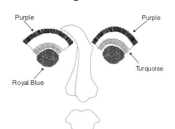

Diagram 5

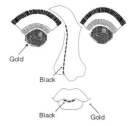

Diagram 6

paper intact. Place the template over the felt, with the outside edges parallel to the edges of the felt (Diagram 1).

2. Make the pattern overlay; see Basic Instructions. Use the overlay to trace all the pattern pieces onto fusible web. Pin the overlay to the felt and leave in place throughout the appliqué process.

3. Cut out 2 fabric pieces for the nose. Peel off the paper backing and place on the felt, fusible side down. The pieces should overlap. Fuse.

4. Working with just a few pieces at a time, cut out and fuse the face, working from the nose out, using the pattern overlay and edge of the template as your guides. Note that space is allowed above and below the eyelids for embroidery. Fuse the rest of the face (Diagram 2). Remove the template.

5. Cut out and fuse the gold, light gold, and gold print rays (Diagram 3), then the light, medium, and dark blue background. Cut out and fuse the purple border pieces (Diagram 4).

Embroider the Details

1. Satin-stitch the eyes with 2 strands of royal blue floss. Satin-stitch below the eyelids with 2 strands of turquoise floss, and above the eyelids with 2 strands of purple floss (Diagram 5).

2. Using 2 strands of gold floss, make small cross stitches for the "shine" in each eye; see photo on page 57. Also make long stitches on the left edges of each eye. Outline-stitch with 2 strands of gold floss on the lips.

3. Using 2 strands of black floss, outline-stitch along the left edge of the yellow nose piece over the dark gold piece. Also outline-stitch with black floss below the center of the mouth (Diagram 6).

4. Using 4 strands of gold floss, make star stitches for the stars in the openings of the blue background.

Frame the Design

Pad the background with 2 layers of polyester fleece. Center the design over the padded background. Have the design framed professionally in a frame with a 10" x 10" opening.

Purple Border   Cut 4

Light Blue   Dark Blue   Dark Rust   Dark Gold   Gold

Medium Blue   Rose   Purple   Gold Print   Yellow

CHAPTER THREE

Table Runner

Materials:

Scraps of cotton fabric; see Step 1
Black felt, 11" wide by the desired finished length
Green felt, 12" wide by the desired length plus 5"
Embroidery floss in these colors: black and tan; see Step 1
$^3/_8$ yard of fusible web
5 assorted buttons
Tracing paper; pencil

Make the Animal Design

1. Select an animal motif from this book for each end of the runner and choose fabrics. If you use the same motif at both ends, be sure to double the amount of fabric. You will also need embroidery floss.

2. Trace the edges of the animal design onto tracing paper. Cut out the animal, leaving the rest of the paper intact. Place the template over the black felt; position as desired.

3. Make the pattern overlay; see Basic Instructions. Use the overlay to trace all the pattern pieces onto fusible web. Pin the overlay to the black felt, with the bottom of the animal 2" from the edge, and leave in place throughout the appliqué process.

4. Cut out fabric pieces for the animal, working with just a few pieces at a time. Peel off the paper backing and place on the felt, fusible side down, using the template as a guide to placement. Fuse the pieces. Repeat to complete the design, following the instructions for the individual animal motif.

5. Pin the template and pattern overlay to the opposite end of the felt. Repeat the cutting and fusing process. Remove the template.

6. Embroider the details; see instructions for individual animals. Place buttons randomly and sew on with black floss.

Finish the Table Runner

1. Trim the black felt to 10" wide. Trim the green felt to 10$^1/_2$" wide and 4$^1/_2$" longer than the black felt piece. Center the black felt over the green felt; pin securely. Buttonhole-stitch the entire edge of the black felt to the green felt, using 3 strands of tan floss.

2. Make a paper pattern for the ends of the green felt. Center and pin to the green felt and cut out. Repeat at the other end.

Woodland Squirrel Pillow

Materials:

Scraps of cotton fabric in these colors: black/white check, gold/black print, brown, gold print, olive, rose, rust, and rust/black check

1 yard of rust/black print fabric; matching thread

13" x 13" piece of black felt

Embroidery floss in these colors: olive, gold, and black

$3/8$ yard of fusible web

$1^3/4$ yards of $1/2$"-diameter cording

16" pillow form

Dressmaker's chalk

Tracing paper; pencil

Make the Squirrel Design

1. Cut out a 9" x 9" piece of tracing paper. Using the pattern on pages 65 and 66, center the paper over the pattern and trace the edges of the squirrel onto it. Cut out the squirrel, leaving the rest of the paper intact. Place the template over the felt, with the outside edges parallel to the edges of the felt (Diagram 1).

2. Make the pattern overlay; see Basic Instructions. Use the overlay to trace all the pattern pieces onto fusible web. Pin the overlay to the felt and leave in place throughout the appliqué process.

3. Cut out fabric pieces for the squirrel's back, working with just a few pieces at a time. Peel off the paper backing and place on the felt, fusible side down, using the template as a guide to placement. Fuse the pieces. Repeat to complete the squirrel's leg, then the arm.

4. Cut out and fuse the squirrel's head, then the neck, body, and feet. Cut out and fuse the squirrel's tail (Diagram 2). Remove the template.

5. Cut out and fuse the olive leaves, then the gold print leaves.

6. Cut out and fuse the rose sections of the acorns. Cut out the rust sections of the acorns. The pieces should touch here, unlike other places in the design. Fuse (Diagram 3).

Embroider the Details

1. Using 2 strands of black floss, satin-stitch the squirrel's eye and nose. Add a single long stitch below the nose (Diagram 4). Sew a running stitch for the veins of the gold print leaves; see photo on page 62.

2. Using 2 strands of gold floss, buttonhole-stitch around selected pieces of the squirrel's body; see photo on page 62.

3. Mark placement for the vines with dressmaker's chalk. Using 4 strands of olive floss, chain-stitch the vines.

Make the Pillow

1. Trim the felt to 11½" x 11½", with the design centered and the edges parallel to the edges of the design.

2. From the rust/black print fabric, cut the following: 1 piece, 15½" x 15½"; 4 pieces, 2½" x 17"; and 2½"-wide strips, piecing as needed to equal 1¾ yards.

Diagram 1

Diagram 2

Diagram 3

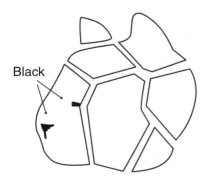

Diagram 4

63

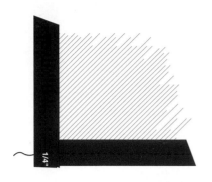

Diagram 5

Diagram 6

Diagram 7

3. Mark the centers of each edge of the felt. Also mark the centers on 1 long edge of each 2½"-wide rust/black print piece. Match the center of the print piece with the edge of the felt. Using a ¼" seam, stitch the purple strip to the edge of the felt, starting and stopping ¼" from each edge of the felt (Diagram 5). Repeat with each edge and the remaining print strips.

4. To miter the corners, fold the right sides of adjacent print pieces together and stitch at a 45-degree angle (Diagram 6). Trim the seam allowance to ¼" and press. Repeat for each corner.

5. To make piping, place the cording in the center of the wrong side of the print bias strip. Fold the bias strip over the cording and stitch close to the cording, using a zipper foot (Diagram 7). Trim the seam allowance ¼" from the stitching line. Place the piping on the right side of the pillow front. Stitch with a ¼" seam, rounding the corners and clipping as needed. Place the pillow front and back right sides together. Stitch the edges together on the stitching line of the piping, stitching as close as possible to the piping and leaving an opening to turn through.

6. Turn the pillow covering right side out, clipping corners as needed to make them smooth. Insert the pillow form. Slipstitch the opening closed.

WOODLAND SQUIRREL PILLOW Pattern

Chain Stitch

WOODLAND SQUIRREL PILLOW Pattern

Chain Stitch

Black/White Check
Gold/Black Print
Gold Print
Olive
Rose
Rust
Rust/Black Check
Brown

Garden Rabbit Pillow

Materials:

Scraps of cotton fabric in these colors: green, aqua, light blue,
    medium blue, lavender print, purple, white, and tan
1 yard of light purple print fabric; matching thread
13" x 13" piece of black felt
Embroidery floss in these colors: white, blue, navy blue, lavender, aqua, and black
$^3/_8$ yard of fusible web
$1^3/_4$ yards of $^1/_2$"-diameter cording
16" pillow form
Tracing paper; pencil

Diagram 1

Diagram 2

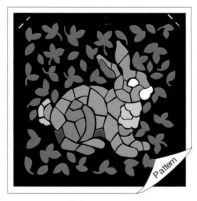

Diagram 3

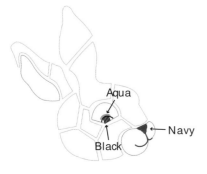

Diagram 4

Make the Rabbit Design

1. Cut a 10" x 10" piece of tracing paper. Using the pattern on pages 69 and 70, center the paper over the pattern and trace the edges of the rabbit onto it. Cut out the rabbit, leaving the rest of the paper intact. Place the template over the felt, with the outside edges parallel to the edges of the felt (Diagram 1).

2. Make the pattern overlay; see Basic Instructions. Use the overlay to trace all the pattern pieces onto fusible web. Pin the overlay to the felt and leave in place throughout the appliqué process.

3. Cut out fabric pieces for the rabbit's head, working with just a few pieces at a time. Peel off the paper backing and place on the felt, fusible side down, using the template as a guide to placement. Fuse the pieces. Repeat to complete the chest, then the body (Diagram 2). Remove the template.

4. Cut out and fuse the leaves, using the template as a guide to placement (Diagram 3). Remove the template.

Embroider the Details

1. Using the pattern for placement and 2 strands of navy floss, satin-stitch the nose. Backstitch the mouth. (Diagram 4).

2. Using 2 strands of black floss, satin-stitch the rabbit's eye. Satin-stitch a small accent above the black with aqua floss.

3. Buttonhole-stitch the edges of selected pieces of blue fabric, using 2 strands of blue floss. Buttonhole-stitch the edges of selected lavender and purple pieces with lavender floss; see photo on page 67.

4. Using 2 strands of white floss, chain-stitch the vine. Make small tack stitches on the edges of most leaves. Couch white floss to the centers of the leaves with tack stitches.

Make the Pillow

1. Trim the felt to 11½" x 11½", with the design centered and the edges parallel to the edges of the design.

2. From the purple print fabric, cut the following: 1 piece, 15½" x 15½"; 4 pieces, 2½" x 17"; and 2½"-wide bias strips, piecing as needed to equal 1¾ yards.

3. Mark the center of each edge of the felt. Also mark the center on 1 long edge of each 2½"-wide purple print piece. Match the center of the purple piece with the edge of the felt. Using a ¼" seam, stitch the purple strip to the edge of the felt, starting and stopping ¼" from each edge of the felt. Repeat with the remaining strips.

4. Refer to Steps 4–6 of the Woodland Squirrel Pillow instructions on page 64.

GARDEN RABBIT PILLOW Pattern

Chain Stitch

Chain Stitch

Green

Aqua

Light Blue

Medium Blue

Lavender Print

Purple

White

Tan

Chain Stitch

Nesting Pair Pillow

Materials:

Scraps of cotton fabric in these colors: light green, green, dark blue,
  gold print, tan, light rust, rust, brown/black print, and brown
1 yard of light green print fabric; matching thread
13" x 13" piece of black felt
Embroidery floss in these colors: black, orange, and gold
$^3/_8$ yard of fusible web
$1^3/_4$ yards of $^1/_2$"-diameter cording
16" pillow form
Tracing paper; pencil

Template

Diagram 1

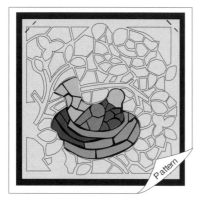

Diagram 2

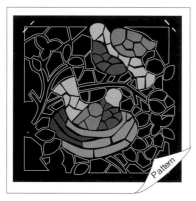

Diagram 3

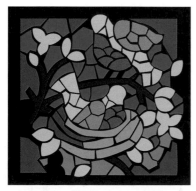

Diagram 4

Make the Bird Design

1. Cut a 10" x 10" piece of tracing paper. Using the pattern on pages 73 and 74, center the paper over the pattern and trace the edges of the nesting bird and nest, and the perching bird. Cut out the nesting bird, leaving the rest of the paper intact. Place the template over the felt, with the outside edges parallel to the edges of the felt (Diagram 1).

2. Make the pattern overlay; see Basic Instructions. Use the overlay to trace all the pattern pieces onto fusible web. Pin the overlay to the felt and leave in place throughout the appliqué process. Cut out fabric pieces for the bird's tail, working with just a few pieces at a time. Peel off the paper backing and place on the felt, fusible side down, using the template as a guide to placement. Fuse the pieces. Repeat to complete the nesting bird and nest (Diagram 2).

3. Cut out the perching bird, leaving the rest of the paper intact. Place the template over the felt, aligning the nesting bird and keeping the outside edges parallel to the edges of the felt.

4. Cut out and fuse the bird's breast. Cut out and fuse the bird's body, tail, and wing (Diagram 3). Remove the template.

5. Cut out and fuse the branch and light green leaves, then the green background. Cut out and fuse the blue background, then the brown background (Diagram 4).

Embroider the Details

1. Using 2 strands of black floss, make a French knot for the birds' eyes, wrapping floss twice around the needle. Sew a running stitch in the gold print sticks of the nest. Buttonhole-stitch the birds' breasts and the top edge of the nest; see photo on page 71.

2. Using 2 strands of gold floss, satin-stitch the perching bird's legs. Satin-stitch the beaks with 2 strands of orange floss.

Make the Pillow

1. Trim the felt to 11½" x 11½", with the design centered and the edges parallel to the edges of the design.

2. From the light green print fabric, cut the following: 1 piece, 15½" x 15½"; 4 pieces, 2½" x 17"; and 2½"-wide bias strips, piecing as needed to equal 1¾ yards.

3. Mark the center of each edge of the felt. Also mark the center on 1 long edge of each 2½"-wide light green print piece. Match the center of the print piece with the edge of the felt. Using a ¼" seam, stitch the purple strip to the edge of the felt, starting and stopping ¼" from each edge of the felt. Repeat with each edge and the remaining print strips.

4. Refer to Steps 4–6 of the Woodland Squirrel Pillow instructions on page 64.

Placement for Branch

NESTING PAIR PILLOW
Pattern

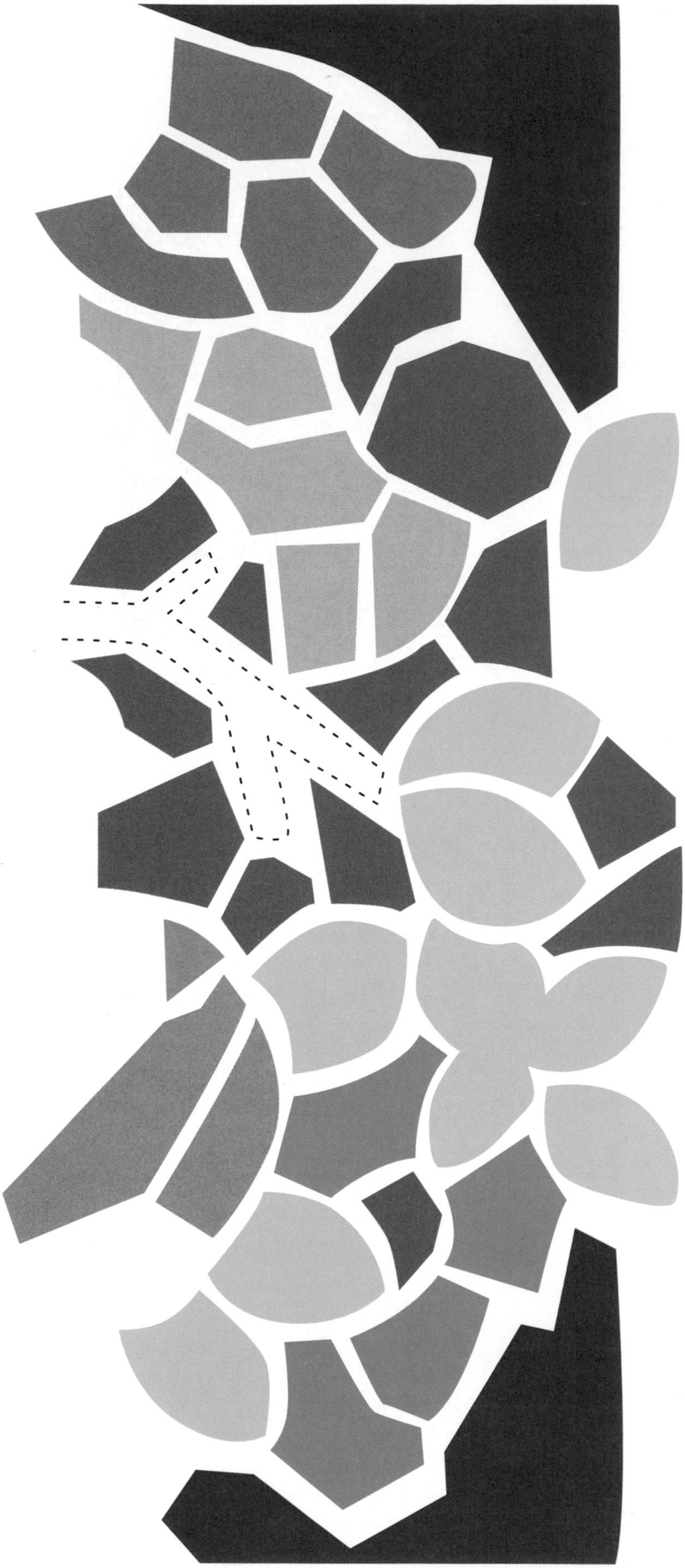

Light Green
Green
Dark Blue
Gold Print
Tan
Light Rust
Rust
Brown/Black Print
Brown

Rainbow Trout Pillow

Materials:

Scraps of cotton fabric in these colors: lavender, gold print, light blue,
   medium blue, medium blue print, green, rust, dark rust, and orange
$^3/_8$ yard of navy blue sport-weight fabric; matching thread
9" x 9" piece of black felt
Black embroidery floss
$^1/_4$ yard of fusible web
$1^1/_4$ yards of navy blue fringe
Polyester stuffing
Tracing paper; pencil

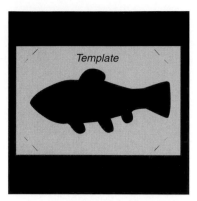

Diagram 1

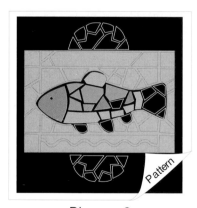

Diagram 2

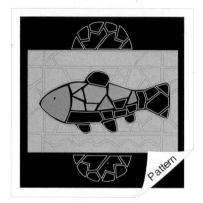

Diagram 3

Make the Fish Design

1. Using the pattern on page 80, trace the edges of the fish and the outside edges of the design onto tracing paper. Cut out the fish shape, leaving the rest of the paper intact. Place the template over the felt, with the outside edges parallel to the edges of the felt (Diagram 1).

2. Make the pattern overlay; see Basic Instructions. Use the overlay to trace all the pattern pieces onto fusible web. Pin the overlay to the felt and leave in place throughout the appliqué process.

3. Cut out the fabric piece for the lavender head. Peel off the paper backing and place on the felt, fusible side down, using the template as a guide to placement. Fuse the piece.

4. Cut out and fuse the gold print body pieces (Diagram 2), then the lavender body pieces.

5. Cut out and fuse the light blue body pieces and light blue fin (Diagram 3).

6. Cut out and fuse the rust body piece and tail pieces. Cut out and fuse the green fins. Remove the template.

7. Cut out and fuse the dark rust background, adding 2 or 3 pieces at a time. Note that the fish head and tail extend into the border (Diagram 4).

8. Cut out and fuse the medium blue pieces, then the medium blue print pieces in the border (Diagram 5).

9. Cut out and fuse the orange pieces in 1 arch. Cut out and fuse the medium blue pieces in the arch. Repeat to complete the second arch (Diagram 6).

10. Make a French knot for the eye of the fish, using 2 strands of black floss wrapped twice around the needle.

Make the Pillow

1. Trim the felt ¼" outside the edge of the design.

2. Cut 2 pieces of navy blue fabric 14" x 10½". Center the fish design on the right side of 1 piece. Pin securely. Slipstitch the edges of the black felt to the navy fabric.

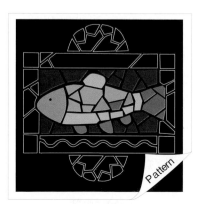

Diagram 4

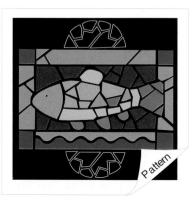

Diagram 5

Diagram 6

3. Place the bound edge of the navy fringe along the edge of the fabric with the loose ends of the fringe toward the center. You may need to ease extra fringe at the corners. Stitch the fringe to the navy fabric.

4. Place the 2 navy pieces right sides together. Stitch the edges together, covering the bound edge of the fringe and leaving an opening in 1 long edge.

5. Turn the pillow covering right side out, clipping the corners as needed to make them smooth. Stuff the pillow firmly. Slipstitch the opening closed.

Striped Bass Pillow

Materials:

Scraps of cotton fabric in these colors: brown, tan stripe, lavender, green print, dark green, royal blue print, light blue, medium blue print, and turquoise

$^3/_4$ yard blue/white checked fabric; matching thread

$^3/_8$ yard gold fabric; matching thread

9" x 9" piece of black felt

$^1/_4$ yard of fusible web

4 tan buttons, $^3/_8$"-diameter

Embroidery floss in these colors: white and gold

$1^1/_2$ yards of small cording

Polyester stuffing

Tracing paper; pencil

Make the Fish Design

1. Using the pattern on page 79, trace the edges of the fish and the outside edges of the design onto tracing paper. Cut out the fish shape, leaving the rest of the paper intact. Place the template over the felt, with the outside edges parallel to the edges of the felt (Diagram 1).

2. Make the pattern overlay; see Basic Instructions. Use the overlay to trace all the pattern pieces onto fusible web. Pin the overlay to the felt and leave in place throughout the appliqué process.

3. Cut out the fabric pieces for the lavender tail, working with just a few pieces at a time. Peel off the paper backing and place on the felt, fusible side down, using the template as a guide to placement. Fuse the pieces. Repeat to complete the tail.

4. Cut out and fuse the tan stripe body pieces (Diagram 2), then the lavender body piece. Cut out and fuse the brown body pieces and head (Diagram 3).

Diagram 1

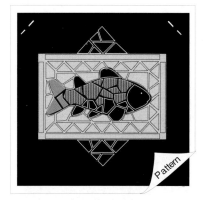

Diagram 2

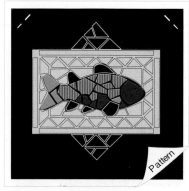

Diagram 3

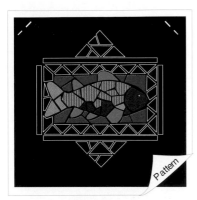

Diagram 4

Diagram 5

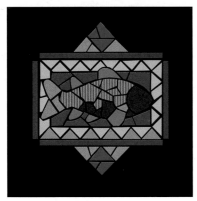

Diagram 6

Diagram 7

5. Cut out and fuse the green fins. Remove the template.

6. Cut out and fuse 2 or 3 pieces of the royal blue print background. Note that the fish head and tail extend into the border. Continue to fuse the background (Diagram 4).

7. Cut out and fuse the light blue pieces in the top and bottom triangles. Cut out and fuse the medium blue print border (Diagram 5). Cut out and fuse the dark green border pieces.

8. Cut out and fuse the medium blue pieces and turquoise pieces in the top triangle. Repeat to complete the bottom triangle (Diagram 6).

9. Make a French knot for the eye of the fish, using 2 strands of white floss wrapped twice around the needle.

Make the Pillow

1. Trim the felt ¹⁄₄" outside the edge of the design.

2. Cut 1 piece of gold fabric 13¹⁄₂" x 10¹⁄₂". Center and pin the fish design to the gold fabric. Sew a running stitch around the design, using 2 strands of gold floss through the felt and gold fabric.

3. Cut 2 pieces of blue/white checked fabric 12¹⁄₂" x 17". Also cut 1¹⁄₄"-wide bias strips, piecing as needed to equal 1¹⁄₂ yards.

4. Center the gold fabric with the fish design on the right side of 1 blue/white checked piece. Pin securely. Turn under ¹⁄₄" and slipstitch the edges of the gold fabric to the checked fabric. Sew 1 button in each corner of the design, using gold thread.

5. To make piping, place the cording in the center of the wrong side of the blue/white checked bias strip. Fold the bias strip over the cording and stitch close to the cording, using a zipper foot (Diagram 7). Trim the seam allowance ¹⁄₄" from the stitching line. Place the piping on the right side of the pillow front. Stitch with a ¹⁄₄" seam, rounding the corners and clipping the seam allowance as needed. Place the right sides of the 2 checked pieces together. Stitch the edges together on the stitching line of the cording, stitching as close as possible to the cording and leaving an opening to turn through.

6. Turn the pillow covering right side out, clipping corners as needed to make them smooth. Stuff the pillow firmly. Slipstitch the opening closed.

STRIPED BASS PILLOW Pattern

Lavender

Green Print

Dark Green

Brown   Tan Stripe

Light Blue

Medium Blue

Royal Blue Print

Turquoise

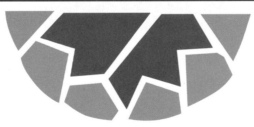

Gold Print		Light Blue		Rust	
Medium Blue Print		Lavender		Dark Rust	
Medium Blue		Green		Orange	

CHAPTER FOUR

Framed Apples

Materials:

Scraps of cotton fabric in these colors: faded red, red, brown, green,
yellow, light blue, and blue-green
15" x 15" piece of purple fabric
9" x 9" piece of black felt
Embroidery floss in these colors: black, light gray, and charcoal
¼ yard of fusible web
10" x 10" piece of polyester fleece
Tracing paper; pencil

Make the Apple Design

1. Using the pattern on page 84, trace the edges of the apples and the outside edges of the design onto tracing paper. Cut out the template along the outside lines. Cut out the apples, leaving the rest of the paper intact. Place the template over the felt, with the outside edges parallel to the edges of the felt (Diagram 1).

2. Make the pattern overlay; see Basic Instructions. Use the overlay to trace all the pattern pieces onto fusible web. Pin the overlay to the felt and leave in place throughout the appliqué process.

3. Cut out the fabric pieces for the apple, working with just a few pieces at a time. Peel off the paper backing and place on the felt, fusible side down, using the template as a guide to placement. Fuse the pieces. Repeat to complete the apples (Diagram 2). Remove the template.

4. Cut out and fuse the light blue background, except outside the branch (Diagram 3). Cut out and fuse the branch, overlapping the apples; see photo on page 82.

5. Cut out and fuse the leaves and remaining light blue background (Diagram 4). Cut out and fuse the blue-green corner pieces.

Embroider the Details

1. Make French knots on the apples with 2 strands of light gray floss wrapped once around the needle, placing them at random; see photo on page 82.

2. Buttonhole-stitch around the outside edges of the apples, using 2 strands of black floss. Buttonhole-stitch the inside edges of the corner pieces, using 2 strands of light gray floss.

3. Trim the felt to 7½" x 7½", or about ¼" outside the design area. Center and pin to the purple fabric. Buttonhole-stitch around the edge of the felt, using 2 strands of charcoal floss.

Frame the Design

Pad the background with a layer of polyester fleece. Center the design over the padded background. Have the design framed professionally in a frame with a 9" x 9" opening.

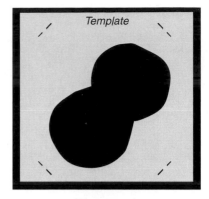

Diagram 1

Diagram 2

Diagram 3

Diagram 4

Faded Red ■ Red ■ Brown ■ Green ■ Yellow ■ Light Blue ■ Blue-Green ■

Framed Grapes

Materials:

Scraps of cotton fabric in these colors: brown, purple, dark
  purple, light blue, light green, and green
15" x 15" piece of purple fabric
9" x 9" piece of black felt
Embroidery floss in these colors: turquoise, white, and charcoal
¼ yard of fusible web
10" x 10" piece of polyester fleece
Tracing paper; pencil

Diagram 1

Make the Grape Design

1. Using the pattern on page 86, trace the edges of the grapes
   and the outside edges of the design onto tracing paper. Cut
   out the template along the outside lines. Cut out the grapes,
   leaving the rest of the paper intact. Place the template over
   the felt, with the outside edges parallel to the edges of the
   felt (Diagram 1).

2. Make the pattern overlay; see Basic Instructions. Use the
   overlay to trace all the pattern pieces onto fusible web. Pin
   the overlay to the felt and leave in place throughout the
   appliqué process.

3. Cut out fabric pieces for the grapes, working with just a few
   pieces at a time. Peel off the paper backing and place on the
   felt, fusible side down, using the template as a guide to
   placement. Fuse the pieces. Repeat to complete the grapes
   (Diagram 2). Remove the template.

4. Cut out and fuse the leaves (Diagram 3), then the branches,
   overlapping the end of 1 branch onto a purple grape.

5. Cut out and fuse the light green tendril, overlapping 1 end
   onto the tip of the leaf. Cut out and fuse the light blue
   background (Diagram 4).

6. Cut out and fuse the light green corner pieces, allowing
   space for chain stitches; see photo on page 82.

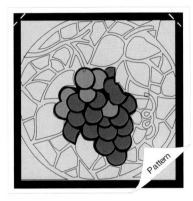

Diagram 2

Embroider the Details

1. Chain-stitch the arcs outside the blue background, using 2
   strands of turquoise floss.

2. Trim the felt to 7½" x 7½", or about ¼" outside the design
   area. Center and pin to the purple fabric. Buttonhole-stitch
   around the edge of the felt, using 2 strands of charcoal floss.

3. Using 2 strands of white floss, satin-stitch the shine on the
   grapes; see pattern.

Diagram 3

Diagram 4

Frame the Design

Pad the background with a layer of polyester fleece. Center the design over the padded background. Have the design framed professionally in a frame with a 9" x 9" opening.

FRAMED GRAPES Pattern

Brown ■   Purple ■   Dark Purple ■   Light Blue ■   Light Green ■   Green ■

Framed Cherries

Materials:

Scraps of cotton fabric in these colors: red, brown, green, light blue, and blue-green

15" x 15" piece of purple fabric

9" x 9" piece of black felt

Embroidery floss in these colors: tan, light gray, and charcoal

$1/4$ yard of fusible web

10" x 10" piece of polyester fleece

Tracing paper; pencil

Template

Diagram 1

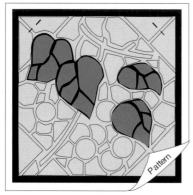

Diagram 2

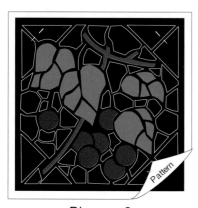

Diagram 3

Diagram 4

Make the Cherry Design

1. Using the pattern on page 89, trace the edges of the 4 leaves and the outside edges of the design onto tracing paper. Cut out the template along the outside lines. Cut out the leaves, leaving the rest of the paper intact. Place the template over the felt, with the outside edges parallel to the edges of the felt (Diagram 1).

2. Make the pattern overlay; see Basic Instructions. Use the overlay to trace all the pattern pieces onto fusible web. Pin the overlay to the felt and leave in place throughout the appliqué process.

3. Cut out fabric pieces for a leaf, working with just a few pieces at a time. Peel off the paper backing and place on the felt, fusible side down, using the template as a guide to placement. Fuse the pieces. Repeat to complete the leaves (Diagram 2). Remove the template.

4. Cut out and fuse the branch, then the cherries (Diagram 3). Cut out and fuse the light blue background (Diagram 4), then the blue-green corner pieces.

Embroider the Details

1. Stem-stitch the stems on the cherries, using 2 strands of tan floss; see photo on page 87.

2. Buttonhole-stitch the inside edges of the corner pieces, using 2 strands of light gray floss.

3. Trim the felt to 7½" x 7½", or about ¼" outside the design area. Center and pin to the purple fabric. Buttonhole-stitch around the edge of the felt, using 2 strands of charcoal floss.

Frame the Design

Pad the background with a layer of polyester fleece. Center the design over the padded background. Have the design framed professionally in a frame with a 9" x 9" opening.

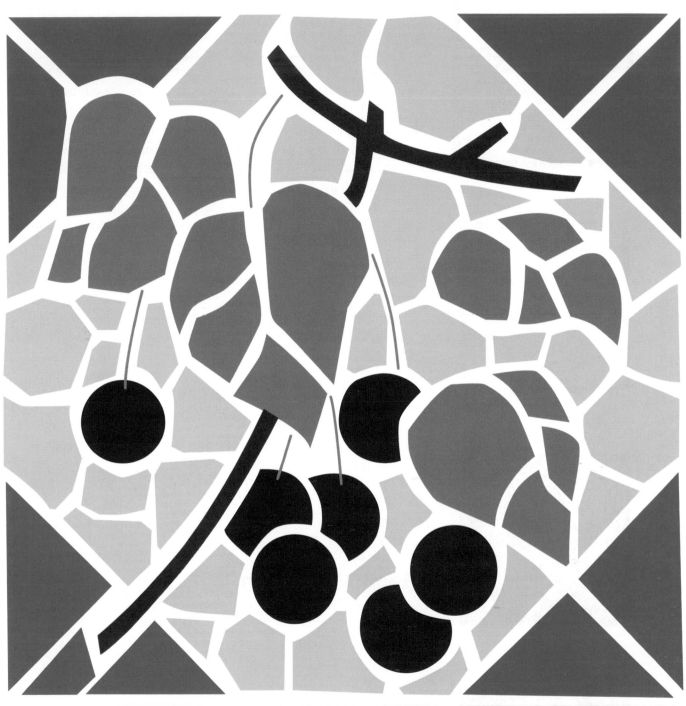

Red	■	Green	■	
Brown	■	Light Blue	■	
		Blue-Green	■	

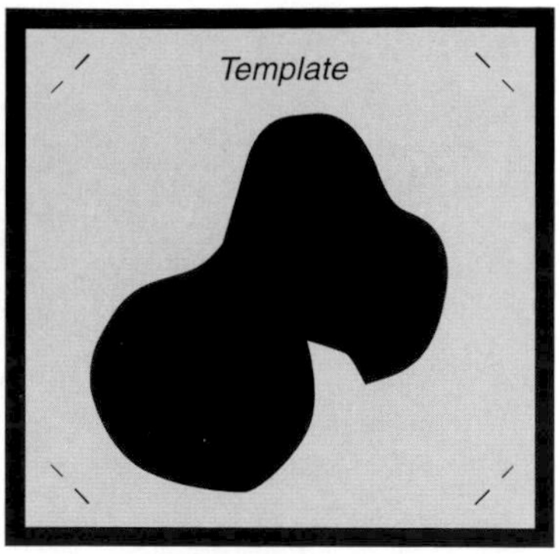

Diagram 1

Framed Pears

Materials:

Scraps of cotton fabric in these colors: brown, purple, light
    blue, green, light gold, gold, gold print, and dark gold
15" x 15" piece of purple fabric
9" x 9" piece of black felt
Embroidery floss in these colors: black, green, and charcoal
$\frac{1}{4}$ yard of fusible web
10" x 10" piece of polyester fleece
Tracing paper; pencil

Diagram 2

Make the Pear Design

1. Using the pattern on page 91, trace the edges of the pears
   and the outside edges of the design onto tracing paper. Cut
   out the template along the outside lines. Cut out the pears,
   leaving the rest of the paper intact. Place the template over
   the felt, with the outside edges parallel to the edges of the
   felt (Diagram 1).
2. Make the pattern overlay; see Basic Instructions. Use the
   overlay to trace all the pattern pieces onto fusible web. Pin
   the overlay to the felt and leave in place throughout the
   appliqué process.
3. Cut out fabric pieces for a pear, working with just a few
   pieces at a time. Peel off the paper backing and place on the
   felt, fusible side down, using the template as a guide to
   placement. Fuse the pieces. Repeat to complete the pears
   (Diagram 2). Remove the template.
4. Cut out and fuse the green leaves (Diagram 3), then the branch.
   Cut out and fuse the light blue background (Diagram 4).
5. Cut out and fuse the purple corner pieces, allowing space
   for chain stitches; see photo on page 87.

Diagram 3

Embroider the Details

1. Buttonhole-stitch around the outside edges of the pears,
   using 2 strands of black floss.
2. Chain-stitch arcs outside the blue background, using 2
   strands of green floss.
3. Trim the felt to $7\frac{1}{2}$" x $7\frac{1}{2}$", or about $\frac{1}{4}$" outside the design
   area. Center and pin to the purple fabric. Buttonhole-stitch
   around the edge of the felt, using 2 strands of charcoal floss.

Frame the Design

Pad the background with a layer of polyester fleece. Center
the design over the padded background. Have the design
framed professionally in a frame with a 9" x 9" opening.

Diagram 4

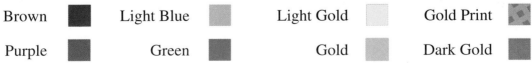

| Brown | ■ | Light Blue | ■ | Light Gold | ■ | Gold Print | ▦ |
| Purple | ■ | Green | ■ | Gold | ■ | Dark Gold | ■ |

Orange Pillow

Materials:

Scraps of cotton fabric in these colors: orange, white,
   brown, green, purple, light blue, and medium blue
$^3/_8$ yard of green print fabric; matching thread
9" x 9" piece of black felt
Embroidery floss in these colors: black, turquoise, yellow,
   and lavender
$^1/_4$ yard of fusible web
$1^1/_2$ yards of black upholstery cording, $^1/_2$"-diameter
Black thread
12" pillow form
Tracing paper, pencil

Make the Orange Design

1. Using the pattern on page 94, trace the edges of the orange and the outside edges of the design onto tracing paper. Cut out the template along the outside lines. Cut out the orange, leaving the rest of the paper intact. Place the template over the felt, with the outside edges parallel to the edges of the felt (Diagram 1).
2. Make the pattern overlay; see Basic Instructions. Use the overlay to trace all the pattern pieces onto fusible web. Pin the overlay to the felt and leave in place throughout the appliqué process.
3. Cut out fabric pieces for the orange, working with just a few pieces at a time. Peel off the paper backing and place on the felt, fusible side down, using the template as a guide to placement. Fuse the pieces. Repeat to complete the orange (Diagram 2). Remove the template.
4. Cut out and fuse the branch, then the leaves. Cut out and fuse the blossoms (Diagram 3).
5. Cut out and fuse the light blue background, then the medium blue background (Diagram 4). Cut out and fuse the purple corner pieces, allowing space for chain stitches; see photo on page 92.

Embroider the Details

1. Buttonhole-stitch around the outside edges of the orange, using 2 strands of black floss.
2. Following the pattern, make French knots on the blossoms with 2 strands of turquoise floss.
3. Using 2 strands of yellow floss, make long stitches. At the end of each long stitch, make a French knot, wrapping the floss once around the needle.
4. Chain-stitch arcs outside the background, using 2 strands of lavender floss.

Make the Pillow

1. Cut 2 pieces of green print fabric 12½" x 12½".
2. Trim the felt to 7½" x 7½", or about ¼" outside the design area. Center and pin to the right side of 1 green print piece. Slipstitch the felt to the green print pillow top.
3. Using a ¼" seam allowance, stitch the edge of the upholstery cording to the edges of the pillow top, rounding the corners and clipping as needed. Place the pillow top and the second green print piece with right sides together. Stitch on the stitching line of the cording, leaving an opening to turn through. Trim the corners. Turn right side out.
4. Insert the pillow form. Slipstitch the opening closed.

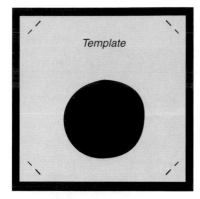

Diagram 1

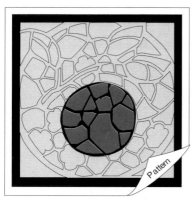

Diagram 2

Diagram 3

Diagram 4

ORANGE PILLOW Pattern

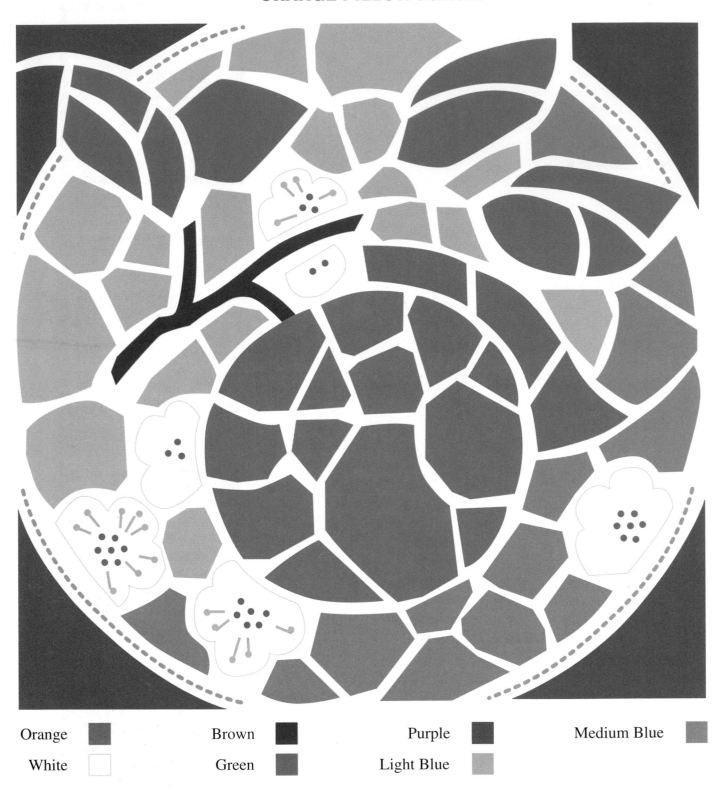

Orange Brown Purple Medium Blue

White Green Light Blue

Lemon Pillow

Materials:
Scraps of cotton fabric in these colors: green, gold, brown, light blue, blue-green, and medium blue

$^3/_8$ yard of green print fabric; matching thread

9" x 9" piece of black felt

Embroidery floss in these colors: black, gold, and blue-gray

$^1/_4$ yard of fusible web

$1^1/_2$ yards of black upholstery cording, $^1/_2$"-diameter

Black thread

12" pillow form

Tracing paper; pencil

Diagram 1

Make the Lemon Design

1. Using the pattern on page 96, trace the edges of the whole lemon and the outside edges of the design onto tracing paper. Cut out the template along the outside lines. Cut out the whole lemon, leaving the rest of the paper intact. Place the template over the felt, with the outside edges parallel to the edges of the felt (Diagram 1).

2. Make the pattern overlay; see Basic Instructions. Trace all the pattern pieces onto fusible web. Pin the overlay to the felt and leave in place throughout the appliqué process.

3. Cut out fabric pieces for the whole lemon, working with just a few pieces at a time. Peel off the paper backing and place on the felt, fusible side down, using the template as a guide to placement. Fuse the pieces. Repeat to complete the whole lemon (Diagram 2). Remove the template.

4. Cut out and fuse the partial lemon. Cut out and fuse the branch, then the leaves (Diagram 3).

5. Cut out and fuse the light blue background, then the medium blue background (Diagram 4). Cut out and fuse the blue-green corner pieces.

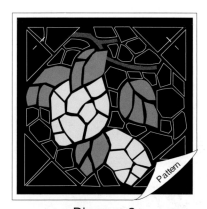
Diagram 2

Embroider the Details

1. Buttonhole-stitch around the outside edges of the lemons, using 2 strands of black floss.

2. Following the pattern, make cross stitches on the lemons, using 2 strands of gold floss. Buttonhole-stitch the inside edges of the corner pieces, using 2 strands of blue-gray floss.

Make the Pillow

Refer to Orange Pillow instructions on page 93.

Diagram 3

Diagram 4

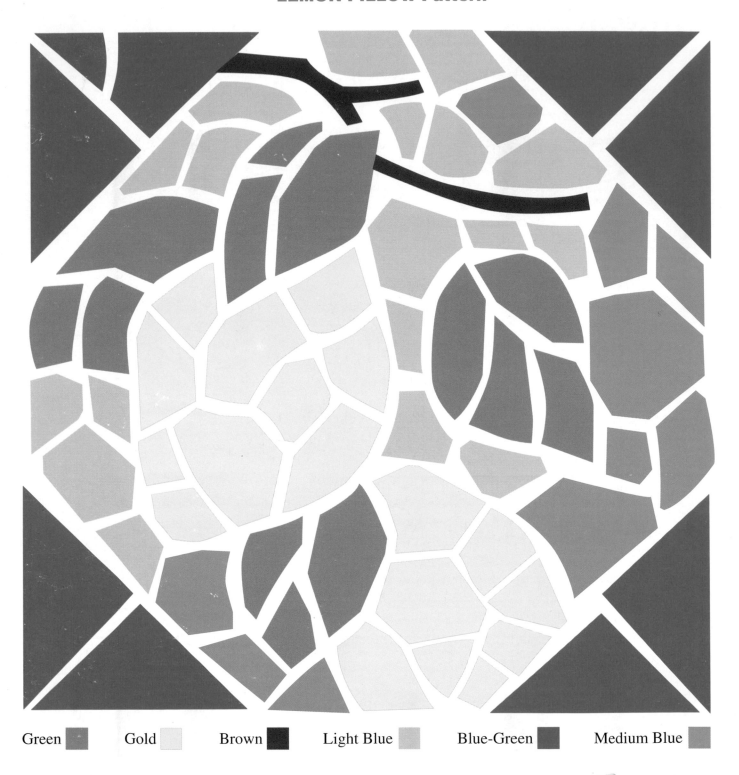

Green Gold Brown Light Blue Blue-Green Medium Blue